CHILD ABUSE

CHILD ABUSE

BY EDWARD F. DOLAN, JR.

FRANKLIN WATTS

NEW YORK/LONDON/
TORONTO/SYDNEY/1980

This book is for Alice and Chet Boddy, good friends.

Library of Congress Cataloging in Publication Data

Dolan, Edward F 1924–
    Child abuse.

    Bibliography: p.
    Includes index.
    SUMMARY: Investigates the various forms
of child abuse and the sources that may be
turned to for help.
    1. Child abuse—United States—Juvenile lit-
erature. 2. Child abuse—United States—Juvenile
literature.   3.   Child   abuse—Services—United
States—Juvenile literature. [1. Child abuse. 2.
Child abuse—Services] I. Title.
HV741.D64   362.7'1   79-26266
ISBN 0–531–02864–X

CONTENTS

ACKNOWL-
EDGMENTS

I am indebted to many people and organizations for their help in the preparation of this book. First, my thanks must go to the following individuals: Congressman John Burton of California; James B. Soetaert, Chief Probation Officer, Marin County, California; Helen Donovan of the National Committee for the Prevention of Child Abuse for her review of the manuscript and for her helpful suggestions; and, for their editorial comment and encouragement, William Royse and Richard B. Lyttle, both of California.

The following organizations most kindly provided me with needed material and with answers to specific questions: The Congressional Research Service of the Library of Congress; the National Center on Child Abuse and Neglect, Department of Health, Education, and Welfare; the American Humane Association; the Child Welfare League of America; the National Center for the Prevention and Treatment of Child Abuse and Neglect; the New York Foundling

Hospital Center for Parent and Child Development; the National Committee for Prevention of Child Abuse. Child Abuse Listening Mediation (CALM); Parental Stress Hotline; Suspected Child Abuse and Neglect (SCAN); Parents Anonymous; and the Citizens Committee for Children and Parents under Stress.

PREFACE

Child abuse is one of the saddest and most tragic problems in the United States today. In all of its forms, it is estimated to affect the lives of between one and two million American children each year. The victims range in age from just a few weeks to their late teens.

Just what are its forms? Basically, there are four:

1. Child beating and neglect
2. Sexual abuse
3. Incest (this is a type of sexual abuse but it is mentioned separately here because of its special nature and because of the particular harm that it seems to do)
4. Exploitation of the child in pornography

As you'll see in chapter 1, child abuse is not new. It has been around for thousands of years. But it is a problem that seems to be especially serious in these troubled times. It is one that thoughtful Americans are concerned about and are trying to solve.

In this book, we're going to be looking at each of the four types of abuse. From there, we'll go on to talk about the why's behind each type of abuse. And then, perhaps most important of all, we'll talk about what many dedicated people are doing to help the victims and their families, in an effort to put an end to the whole tragedy.

But, one point must be made right at the start. While this book is about a great many people who are in trouble—both children and adults—I do not want to leave the impression that *all* American families mistreat their children in some way. This is not the case. Our country abounds with loving families. They are in the great majority. To give the impression that all Americans abuse their children is to do a grave injustice to the countless fine families that make up the heart of our nation.

This book has a very simple purpose—to encourage and inspire you to be of help. Child abuse in all its forms is a problem that must be solved. The solution will require the thinking and the sympathetic effort of everyone, no matter how young or old.

CHILD ABUSE

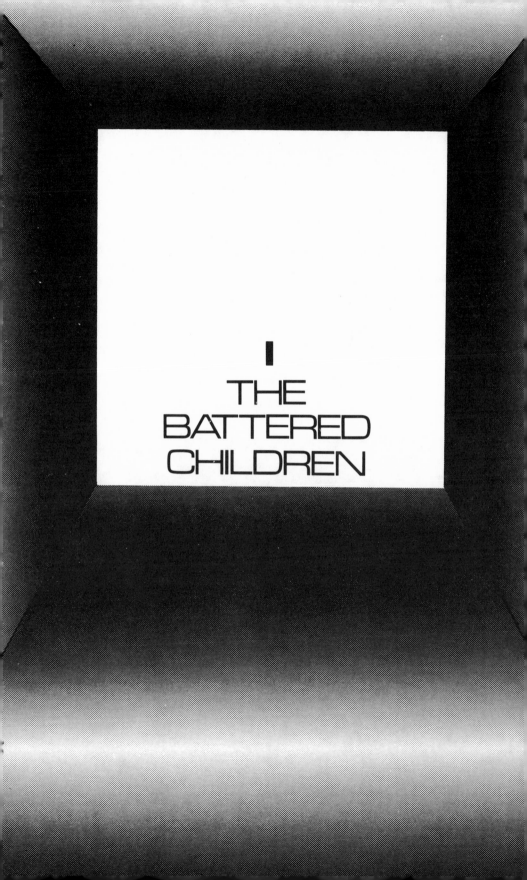

I
THE
BATTERED
CHILDREN

When I was nine years old, I went out to play in new trousers. My father wanted me to change into an old pair first, but I was in a big hurry and dashed off with the promise that I'd be careful. I took a tumble while climbing a fence and the new trousers ended up with a torn knee. And I ended up with a smack across the rear when my father saw what had happened.

I'll never forget that smack because it was as close as I ever came to a real spanking. I was one of the world's lucky kids. My parents didn't believe in spankings. It wasn't that my folks weren't strict; they were. But they didn't think it was right to hit a child. Nor did they think that it did much good.

Most children today are just as lucky as I was. When they do something wrong, their parents may bawl them out. They may take away some privileges or assign extra jobs around the house. And sometimes they may turn to a spanking or a swat when they think it's needed or when they've been pushed too far. At no time, though, are the kids in danger of being injured or killed.

But some youngsters aren't so lucky. For example, take the case of two sisters—let's call them Patty and Joan—from Akron, Ohio.

A worried neighbor called the police about them some months ago. Officers went to their home and found that four-year-old Patty had a hole in her lip. One toe was missing. There were numerous scars all over her body. She had cuts so deep that the bones were showing.

Twelve-year-old Joan was hurt just as badly. The officers saw that part of one ear was missing. She had a broken arm that had never been set. There were scars on her hands, back, and neck. The officers said that she and Patty had been beaten time and again by their stepfather. He'd used a belt and a shovel.

What happened to the two sisters was frightening. Fortunately, it's not the sort of thing that happens to the lucky majority of children. But it does happen to many youngsters. Far, far too many, the authorities say.

AN AMERICAN DISGRACE

According to social agencies, the beatings of children have been multiplying over the past twenty years. (There has also been an increase in all types of child abuse during that time.) These are beatings that go far beyond what anyone could ever call a swat across the rear or a spanking. They're beatings that have cruelly injured their victims— sometimes for life. Some have even ended in death.

Child abuse in its many forms has been a sad fact of life since history began. But today's beatings are so numerous that many doctors believe that they have reached "epidemic" proportions in the United States. The victims have even come to have a special name of their own. They're known as battered children.

4

The term originated in the early 1960s when Dr. C. Henry Kempe of Denver, Colorado, used it in a speech. After years of treating abused children, he was speaking at a meeting of the American Academy of Pediatrics. He also used the name in a book, *The Battered Child,* that he wrote with Dr. Ray Helfer, in 1968. The book was widely read, and the term became a familiar part of our language.

Since then, concerned Americans have been asking questions about these children. Four questions always top the list:

How many children are being beaten?
How are they beaten?
Who are these battered children?
Why is the number of beatings increasing in our country?

Though we know that many youngsters are as cruelly treated as Patty and Joan, we don't know the exact number. It's a number that we could get only if all the cases of abuse in the country were reported to the authorities. But most cases go unreported and remain secret within the families involved. It's estimated that less than 50 percent are ever reported to the proper authorities.

But the reported cases can give us some idea of how bad things are. In the early 1970s, a U.S. government survey showed that 60,000 cases were being reported each year. By 1976, the annual total had passed a half-million.

Not every one of those half-million cases involved a different child. Many were repeats, with the same victims being reported again and again as they were beaten anew. Keeping this in mind, the government has figured that at least 100,000 to 200,000 young Americans are being regularly and severely battered each year. Attacking them are their parents, stepparents, and guardians.

Another kind of estimate comes from Dr. Vincent Fontana, who has long helped the abused children brought to

New York City's Foundling Hospital. Deeply troubled, he has watched the beatings multiply over the years. In 1973, he warned that the nation's doctors could expect to treat at least 1.5 million victims in the next five to ten years if the increase continued at a steady rate. He added that 300,000 of those victims would be permanently injured, either physically or emotionally.

Dr. Fontana also predicted that some 50,000 children would die of the abuse over the five- to ten-year period. At present, the federal government reports that all forms of abuse are claiming 2,000 young lives a year.

The death toll makes abuse the number five killer of children in the United States. Running just ahead of it are: (1) accidents, (2) cancer, (3) inherited physical and mental defects, and (4) pneumonia.

Some doctors think that abuse may soon pass some of the above killers. Unless stopped, they say, it stands a good chance of becoming the leading killer of the nation's young. Dr. Fontana believes that it's already taken over that spot.

Many battered children must endure a second terrible problem—neglect. Neglect was seen when Baltimore police went to nine-year-old Betty's home on a tip. They found her locked in a clothes closet and scarred from many beatings. The girl had been kept in there for half her life while her parents ignored her as they went about their daily business. She was covered with filth and weighed only 23 pounds (10.35 kg).

Neglect, which may accompany the beatings or be there without them, means that the parents fail to take care of a child in any of several ways.

For instance, there is physical neglect when they fail to provide adequate food, clothing, and shelter. There is emotional neglect when they refuse to give their love. Educational neglect when they don't see to it that the child goes to school. And moral neglect when they let the child run loose in the streets at all hours so that he or she risks getting into trouble with the law.

The federal government estimates that about 700,000 children in the country are neglected to one degree or another.

By checking the reported cases, we can come up with no more than a general idea of the total number of children being beaten. But the reported cases can give us a very clear picture of *how* they're being battered. The attacks are brutal. The weapons are frightening.

Patty and Joan's stepfather used a belt and a shovel. Some adults have attacked with their fists and feet. Some have whipped the children with chains, ropes, electric cords, leather straps, or canes. Some have clubbed them with baseball bats, wooden sticks, or broom handles. Others have poured scalding water or coffee over them.

Some children have been thrown against walls or down flights of stairs. Others have been shaken until they've suffered brain damage or a form of whiplash. Some have had their hands held down on hot stoves or against steaming pipes. One little girl was made to sit on a hot radiator as punishment whenever she wet herself.

Beatings such as these can permanently injure many of the children. For instance, a five-year-old boy was recently brought to a Georgia hospital by his parents. His cheek bone was broken, and there was blood pouring from one eye. His parents claimed that he had fallen downstairs.

But the hospital doctors were suspicious. They questioned the parents closely. Finally, the father admitted the truth. He had lost his temper and had lashed out with his fist when his son wouldn't obey him. The eye was so badly damaged that it had to be removed.

Many of the beatings have ended in emotional damage. Doctors at a Florida hospital saw this kind of injury when a two-year-old girl was brought to them. There was no expression in her eyes. She didn't want to talk or eat. She wouldn't play with the toys that were put on her bed. She refused to make friends with any adult.

The doctors soon found the reasons for her condition. She had been continually beaten at home and had been made to watch while her father had whipped her baby brother. It is possible, the doctors say, that the damage done to her will last a lifetime.

Another case of emotional abuse concerns an eleven-year-old boy. He was never actually touched by his "attacker." An orphan, Bobby lived with his aunt. Whenever her women friends came to visit, she made him take off all his clothes. Then he had to parade in front of everyone.

The boy told police that he wished his aunt had beaten him instead. It was his spirit as well as his body that had been abused.

Other children may be emotionally abused without ever being touched. They may be yelled at too often. Or they may be criticized too much and too harshly. Though they don't have a single scar on the outside, they're still considered to be abused—the victims of attacks that may plague them for years to come.

WHO ARE THE BATTERED CHILDREN?

They are, first, children of all ages. No child is too young to be safe from abuse. Dawn proves the point.

Bleeding and ill, Dawn was brought to a South Carolina hospital, where all efforts to save her life failed. When an autopsy was performed, doctors found that she had fourteen broken ribs, a broken knee, and a ruptured liver and spleen. It was also found that she had alcohol in her bloodstream. Her father was arrested for murder. Dawn was six weeks old at the time of her death.

At the opposite end of the scale is Linda. Her parents were angry because they didn't like her friends. When she came home late one night, her father held her down while her mother slapped her and then scratched her face with long fingernails. Linda was sixteen years old.

Dawn's case horrifies everyone, but Linda's comes as a surprise to many people. There is a widespread belief that teen-agers are pretty safe from abuse. It's felt that they're big enough and old enough to defend themselves against attack or to escape by running away.

Doctors at Children's Hospital in Washington, D.C., say they've been treating more and more teen-agers as the years go by. From 1973 to 1974, only nine teen-age cases were brought in for care. From 1975 to 1976, the cases were up to thirty-six. The average age of the victims was thirteen, but the majority of battered children are much younger. Studies show that those most badly injured are usually under the age of three. Most deaths occur in children under five, with the greatest number centering on babies not yet one year old.

Among younger children, boys are most often the victims. But, by age eleven, things begin to turn around and the girls take the lead. By age sixteen and seventeen, girl victims outnumber the boys two to one.

Not only are the battered children of all ages, but they also come from all types of homes. There was a time when most reports of abuse came from the poorest neighborhoods. But now there is an increasing number of reports from middle-class and wealthy neighborhoods, in all parts of the country.

And one other thing must be said. This book is about child abuse in the United States. But that doesn't mean that the problem affects only Americans. Abuse is also a problem in other countries—and it seems to be growing there just as much as it is here.

For instance, seven hundred children are battered to death in England each year. Another four hundred are left with permanent brain damage. The figures are even worse in

9

Germany, with a thousand deaths a year. Germany has the highest rate of child abuse in Europe.

At this point, we come to the fourth question that people are asking: Why is the number of beatings on the increase in our country? It's the question that opens the next chapter and sets us to looking at the kinds of parents who batter their children.

2
WHY?

No one actually knows for certain why child abuse is on the increase. But many experts in child care think that the terrible pressures of our century are at least partially to blame.

We live in troubled times, some experts say. The threat of nuclear holocaust looms constantly over us. There is political unrest throughout the world. Industry is destroying our natural resources. The family unit seems to be falling apart as the divorce rate goes on rising; and let's not forget the "generation gap" that now divides the young and old in so many families.

Faced with these tensions, many people can feel their nerves being stretched to—and beyond—the breaking point. Seeking relief, they may hit out at someone close by. Too often, that someone is a child.

There has always been child abuse in the world because of the ignorance and cruelty in some adults. But now, the pressures of modern times are only adding to the problem.

They're driving people, who might otherwise never think of hurting a child, to join with the ignorant and the cruel.

Though the "troubled times theory" makes sense, there are many other experts who disagree with it.

They argue that there were just as many battered and abused children before the turn of the century, as there are now. It's just that the general public didn't hear very much about them. Now, thanks mostly to the work of such people as Drs. Kempe and Fontana, the beatings have been given much press and television coverage.

The public has been outraged by what it's seen. All the states have taken action. They've passed laws calling for all cases of abuse to be reported to the authorities. And so, the experts say, there have been more reports turned in than ever before. What we're seeing is not an increase in the beatings themselves. Rather, it's an increase in *the number of reports*.

Dr. Fontana doesn't go along with this view. He is sure that the actual number of beatings is up. As proof, he says that New York City is now seeing two children beaten to death a week. Things weren't this bad ten or more years ago, he adds flatly.

In a later chapter, we'll be talking more about the laws that have led to the increase in reports.

SOME BASIC FACTS

We may never learn for certain which of these views is the right one. There is some truth in each of them. And they both agree on one point: Child abuse is one of the country's biggest problems.

But there are some things that we do know for certain. Recent studies have revealed a string of facts about the people who batter their children.

For instance, it's been found that most abusive parents don't "team up" against the child. Abuse is usually the work of just one parent, even though the other may well know that it's taking place.

Sometimes, though, the other parent doesn't know what's going on. Away at the office all day, a father may never see a beating and will believe the story that his wife invents to cover her tracks—that their son was hurt in a fall from his bike. Often, the son won't speak up because he is afraid or loves his mother too much to do so. A long time may pass before the father learns the truth.

Sometimes, the other parent sees the beatings but does nothing to interfere. Often, a mother fears that the enraged father will turn on her. Or fears that he'll storm out of the house and desert the family.

Another fact has been firmly established: Though some abusive parents are cruel by nature, most are not. Nor are most psychotic; fewer than 10 percent have been found to be emotionally or mentally ill. Most are ordinary, hard-working people.

Further, it's safe to say that most genuinely love their children. "This may seem strange, but it's still true," a doctor friend of mine says. "I see it all the time."

My friend works at a San Francisco hospital. "You should be there when they bring in a hurt child. The parents are usually pale and shaken. The mother may be crying. They'll be holding the child and saying comforting things to him. You can see that they're not fooling. They're really upset. . . ."

It's also been learned that many parents shower the children with affection and extra care between beatings. They feed them especially well. They keep them very clean —thoroughly scrubbed and neatly dressed.

"It's easy to see what they're doing," my friend says. "They're trying to make up for things . . . trying to tell the youngster that they love him . . . trying to wipe out an awful feeling of guilt. . . ."

If all this is true—if most abusive parents are ordinary

15

people who genuinely love their children—then what drives them to the beatings?

The studies have come up with many answers. To begin, as ordinary as the parents may be, they all have problems or personal weaknesses that make them dangerous. Drinking too much is one especially dangerous problem.

ALCOHOLISM

In 1976, the American Humane Association made a study of 357,533 cases of abuse and neglect from across the country. The association, which has long worked for the rights and welfare of children, found that alcohol was involved in 14 percent of the cases of abuse. And it was involved in 18.5 percent of the cases of neglect.

Drinking parents may be alcoholics—people who turn to alcohol so much that their need for it is seen as an illness. Or they may only drink from time to time, but be the sort who become mean when they've drunk too much.

Both types can be dangerous, but alcoholics are considered the more dangerous. Their drunkenness looms as a constant threat to the well-being of the children. The harm that can be done is seen in a story from Detroit.

There, police found a six-year-old girl tied to her bed so that she wouldn't be able to wander off while her parents were out drinking. The child said that her mother and father had been doing this for "a long time"—for as long as she could remember—and had never got her a babysitter. This time, they had been gone all night before worried neighbors called the police.

The children of people with any sort of an alcohol problem don't just run the risk of abuse and neglect. Even when there isn't out-and-out abuse or neglect, there can be other troubles.

For instance, studies show that many children feel rejected and unwanted when their parents seem to forget all about them while drinking. Many are embarrassed by their parents and are afraid of what friends and neighbors will think. And many are upset because life is always changing around the house. One day, the parents are sober and things are great. But the next day. . . .

Older children face an extra burden. Often, they must take over the house and care for their younger brothers and sisters. They're forced into being parents. It's a job that can make life miserable by interfering with school and all other outside activities. Worse yet, the older children must often become parents to their parents, cleaning up after them and feeding them during the period of sobering up.

Experts in child care say that any of these problems can cause the youngsters to develop emotional and behavioral problems of their own—now or in the future. There is then the danger that the children themselves will end up drinking heavily in later life.

Parents who are drug users are considered to be as dangerous as alcoholics. Social workers say that the big problem here is neglect because drugs can cut so deeply into the parents' ability to look after the youngsters. It's also known that some users start their children on drugs.

OVERDISCIPLINE

Practically everyone agrees that some discipline is necessary if the child is to learn right from wrong. But some parents carry the idea of discipline to a savage degree. The results can be tragic.

The staff at a midwestern hospital recently had a look at what brutal discipline can do. It happened when sixteen-month-old Donnie's father brought him in with an ear injury. On being questioned, the father said that the ear had been hurt while he was teaching Donnie to obey. Every time the child failed to come when called, the father walked over and gave Donnie's ear a "gentle tug"—those were the father's words. The father didn't seem to know just how strong he was. Those "gentle tugs" had torn the ear partially away from the head.

IMMATURITY

Some children suffer abuse because the mother or father is simply too young or immature for all the work, responsibilities, and problems that go with being a parent.

One of the greatest dangers is that very young and energetic parents won't be able to stand the duties that keep them tied to the house. A case in point comes from a seventeen-year-old mother in California. Her baby was sickly and always crying and requiring attention.

"I loved my baby. Really I did," the young mother recalls. "But I wanted a little freedom to get out and see my friends and have a good time. . . . But she wouldn't let me. . . . I was so tired . . . and there was all that crying. . . .

"I wouldn't have hurt my baby for the world. But one day . . . I don't know what happened. . . . I just couldn't take it anymore. . . . I just started slapping her again and again and telling her to shut up. I cut her lip and made it bleed."

Often the parent is so young and he or she has yet to learn the simplest things about child rearing. A young mother in Georgia brought her child to the hospital after she had injured him badly with a spanking. She admitted that she had spanked the baby to make him stop crying. She was surprised when the doctors told her that spankings will never stop a baby's cries.

THE GENERATION GAP

The "generation gap"—that great difference in the way that adults and teen-agers see things—seems to be behind much of the trouble when older parents are involved. Two stories from Los Angeles prove the point.

18

Thirteen-year-old Steve didn't see anything wrong with smoking marijuana. But his family did. His father flew into a rage when he found three joints hidden in the boy's room. He hit Steve and knocked him unconscious.

Deborah's parents very much wanted her to go to college when she graduated from high school. Deborah couldn't have cared less. At sixteen, she came home one afternoon and said that she was going to be married instead—to a boy that her mother couldn't stand. Her mother knocked her down and then sat on her and slapped her face repeatedly.

These two cases were handled by a young psychologist. He says: "I don't think that anyone is the villain here. Not the parents. Not the kids. It's just that they're all caught up in an explosive situation that they don't know how to handle. . . .

"The parents are angered and worried by the kids' new ideas of how life should be lived. They're all ideas so different from the ones the parents were raised with. As for the kids, they think the parents are out of date and trying to hold them back. . . .

"It would be nice if everyone—kids and parents alike—tried to talk quietly, tried to understand the other person's point of view. But they don't. Then there's trouble and somebody gets hurt."

Of course, the generation gap isn't alone in causing trouble. Older parents have battered their teen-agers for other reasons. One emotionally disturbed mother admitted that she beat her daughter because she was jealous of her youthful looks. A father admitted that he was furious and heartbroken because his son was girlish in manner. Another mother was embarrassed by her daughter's fatness.

THE GREATEST CAUSE

By far the greatest number of beatings come from parents who have trouble handling life's everyday problems. On the outside, they may seem to be perfectly healthy, normal people. But on the inside, they quickly boil over when faced with stress and frustration. Other people may be able to control themselves when up against the very same things. But not these parents.

Any sort of problem can cause trouble here. It can be a small one. Some fathers have lashed out after a bad day at the office or a hard time coming home in traffic. One mother lost her temper and hit her son because she had a throbbing headache. Quite often, it's a growing collection of minor pressures that finally breaks the parent.

Or the problem can be a big one. A twelve-year-old boy was always being scolded and slapped for playing his records too loud and not hanging up his clothes; all this happened while his parents were fighting between themselves and talking about getting a divorce. A father viciously spanked his ten-year-old daughter on the day that he lost his job. Studies show that cases of abuse always go up in times of joblessness or when the parents are too deeply in debt.

Whatever the problems—large or small—they finally prove to be too much. Frustrations boil over into rage. Mother or Dad strikes out at the youngster.

One fact doesn't help matters at all. Studies have found that most abusive parents usually have few—if any—friends in the neighborhood. Also, they usually don't belong to church, social, or civic groups. And often they don't have any strong ties with their own parents or with other relatives; they may be angry with them or live too far away.

All this means that they have no one to talk to in times of stress. And no activities that will take their minds off their problems. With no way to "let off steam," it's doubly hard to keep the pressures of everyday life under control.

Parents who can't handle their frustrations come from every walk of life. Included in their number are the people we've already talked about—the parent troubled by the pressures of our century, the drinking or drug-addicted parent, the too-young parent, and the parent caught in the generation gap.

20

Some of the parents are prosperous, even wealthy. They may seem to have everything that anyone would ever want. But the father may be working too hard and worrying too much about getting ahead in his career. Both parents may be worried about paying for a large home and sending the kids to an expensive college. Both may be worried about their social standing in the neighborhood.

And some parents are poor, even poverty-stricken. All experts agree that abuse is always a great danger in deprived neighborhoods. Families are forced to live in cramped conditions. The parents can neither make a decent living nor have the many good things that other people own and enjoy. The future looks as hopeless as the present.

In either case, the families are set up for trouble, with the child as the victim.

WHEN THEY WERE CHILDREN

"I've found that many abusive parents have one thing in common. They were abused themselves as kids."

The speaker is my doctor friend at the San Francisco hospital. He is not alone in what he has seen. A study made at the University of Colorado School of Medicine found the same thing. About 80 percent of all abusive parents were once abused children.

"What else can you expect?" my friend asks. "They were raised in a violent atmosphere. Their folks never taught them to be gentle and patient people. And so they're going to be violent when things go wrong. They're not going to be gentle and patient because they never learned how."

For these same reasons, my friend adds, you can expect most of today's abused children to grow up and abuse their own children. "It's a vicious circle," he says. He knows of one study that found a family in which the youngsters had been abused for four generations.

There's another reason why a mistreated child is apt to become an abusive parent. The doctor explains:

"He's deprived of love and warmth as a child. These are things that we all want and need. When he becomes a parent, he looks for them in his own children. But perhaps the kids don't give them to him—either not at all or not as much as he wants. Perhaps they misbehave and talk back. Perhaps they have interests that take them out of the house. Whatever the case, he feels cheated. And so he lashes out—just the way his parents lashed out at him when he was young."

The doctor goes on to one more fact. Abuse doesn't just mean that the child is likely to become an abusive parent. There's another great danger.

Studies show that abused children have the habit of getting into trouble with the law—now or in the future. A study of ninety murderers in Texas and Minnesota prisons reported that all had been victims of child abuse. A University of South Carolina study found that the same thing was true of nearly all the young people in the state's correctional system.

In this chapter, we've looked at the main reasons for child abuse. There are many others that are not quite so common.

For instance, one father admitted beating his son because he had wanted a daughter instead. A mother said that she mistreated her twins because she had never wanted to have children. Another spanked her son whenever he did things that reminded her of the bad habits that she couldn't stand in her husband.

It's time now to move on to two other questions: What is being done to help these children? And to help the parents who want to overcome this problem that is making life so terrible in their homes?

Before we can answer these questions, we need to take a look at the history of child abuse.

3
A HISTORY
OF
CHILD ABUSE

There is nothing new about child abuse. In many ancient tribes, the people killed every fourth or fifth newborn infant. This was done so that there would never be too many mouths for the tribe's meager food supply. Early people also sacrificed their children to the gods in the hope of bringing good fortune or good harvests.

In later times, poverty-stricken parents in many parts of the world sold their children into slavery. There were even families who maimed their sons and daughters—breaking their legs or gouging out an eye—so that the youngsters would arouse great pity when they were sent out to work as beggars. Here in America, black children were raised in slavery. Early in our industrial era, white children worked long hours for next to nothing in factories and mines.

One such worker was Melissa Owens. When she was a grandmother in the late nineteenth century, she wrote of her experiences as a child on the East Coast. She recalled that she had gone to work at age eight in a mill. Her shift began at dawn and ran for ten hours, six days a week.

One day, she hurt her hand so badly on a loom that a bone in her little finger had to be removed. The mill refused to pay her for the working time she had lost while going to the doctor.

Melissa did not think that her parents had mistreated her by sending her to work at such an early age. Her family was poor, as were all the families around her. Everyone—even the very young—had to help put food on the table. The parents weren't to blame, she said. At fault were the times, which allowed employers to exploit their workers.

EARLY CASES

If child abuse is old, then so is the worry that it has caused many people. Here in America, their concern was seen before we were yet a nation. Sometime in the mid-seventeenth century, a New England man was made to stand trial for murder. He had so severely punished a boy who worked for him that the youngster had died. The man was sentenced to death.

A few years later, another man was found guilty of causing the death of a servant boy. The verdict was manslaughter. As punishment, the judge ordered that the man's hands be burned and that all his possessions be taken from him.

Both these cases concerned children whose families had sent them out to be servants or apprentices. It was common practice to send the youngsters out this way, not only here in America but in many other parts of the world. In a day before universal education, it enabled young people to learn a trade or a business. But mistreatment was common, especially when a youngster didn't learn fast enough or wasn't obedient enough to suit a harsh master. In 1700, the colony of Virginia passed a series of laws to protect young servants and apprentices against mistreatment.

As time went on, other efforts were made to protect children. For instance, there were the almshouses of the eighteenth and nineteenth centuries. They were meant for children whose poverty-stricken parents couldn't—or wouldn't—support them. Here, in institutions supported by charitable donations from the public, the children were to be fed and cared for.

But the almshouses—especially those in the big cities—could be worse than the homes from which the children came. Many were filthy. The treatment was apt to be harsh. The food was bad. And, on top of all else, the places weren't meant just for children. Adults were sent there as well. Many were thieves and professional beggars who quickly turned the youngsters into criminals.

Through the years since, a number of steps have been taken to safeguard children against these and other abuses. We now have laws that govern how institutions for the young must be operated. There are laws to protect children who are put up for adoption and laws to keep the young from growing up without an education. There are laws to help needy children and laws to protect children against the terrible labor practices of the past, thus making it impossible for employers to treat the young like slaves.

Although this has been fine progress, it has mainly been directed against having children go hungry or be mistreated by the public.

We've been much slower in taking steps to safeguard the young against abuse by their own parents. There have been three reasons for this slowness. The first is a legal one.

A LEGAL PROBLEM

Our law in the United States is based on British common law. When British common law first took shape centuries ago, it gave the father virtual control over his children. It left him to raise and discipline them in any way that he thought correct. He could do practically anything that he wished with them, including selling them.

In the eighteenth and nineteenth centuries, America's

political leaders stuck pretty close to British common law in all their legislation. They were willing to pass laws against some forms of child abuse. But they wouldn't allow any law to interfere with the parents' right to rear their children as they saw fit within the privacy of the home.

It must be said here that some local authorities—especially if they were Puritans—didn't totally agree with the lawmakers. In early New England, the town courts brought in several parents and told them that their homes were "unsuitable" for children. The children were then taken away.

The removals had nothing to do with abuse. Rather, the parents were found guilty of not giving their young a "proper religious upbringing" or not teaching them the value of hard work. One father had his children taken away because he never went to church on the Sabbath.

Much British common law still remains with us today. Parents still have the right to raise their children as they think best. But, thanks to the advances in thinking made through the years, our law has come to concentrate as much on the responsibilities of parenthood. The parents must provide the child with proper care, food, shelter, clothing, and medical treatment. They may not hurt the child or deprive him or her of the necessities of life.

TWO THOUGHTS

The other two reasons for the slow action against child abuse have to do with beliefs that people once held about children and families.

First, many of the people of the eighteenth and nineteenth centuries firmly believed that every parent loved and took good care of his or her child. They would admit that a cruel employer might mistreat a boy or a girl. But a parent? Impossible. It went against nature.

To these people, the idea of abuse by a parent was so repulsive that they couldn't bring themselves to think about

28

it. When they saw reports of abuse in the newspapers, they refused to believe them.

Oddly enough, the second idea seems almost the exact opposite of the first. But it was just as widely believed—and often by the very same people. It held that physical punishment was necessary to keep a child from becoming a brat, a delinquent, or a lazy worker. The language of the day gave us a number of sayings that are still with us:

"Spare the rod and spoil the child."

"He needs a pat on the back—pretty far down."

"A good spanking never hurt anyone."

This belief made it difficult for many people to take seriously the beatings they heard about. They thought that perhaps the parent had been doing nothing more than a good job of disciplining. Or perhaps the child had "asked for it." Or perhaps the beating had been given out of love, to keep the child from doing wrong in the future.

Together, these two beliefs—which are still held by many people today—kept a great segment of the American public from seeing just how bad some cases of abuse were. There then could be no nationwide demand for laws to change things.

And something else must be said. Press coverage of abuse wasn't as great as it is today. Newspapers weren't as large. There was no radio and no television. So, countless people never spoke out against abuse simply because they knew nothing of it.

But, despite all these problems, there was some progress made. One of the most important early steps was taken just over one hundred years ago.

In 1870, a church worker in New York City was sickened when she saw what was happening to a ten-year-old named Mary Ellen Wilson. Mary Ellen, who lived in a slum neighborhood, was being starved and continually beaten. The church worker begged the police to remove the child to safety. But no one could do a thing because there were no local or state laws to cover the situation. Nor were there any at the federal level.

Then the worker had an idea. She went to see Eldridge T. Gerry of the New York Society for the Prevention of Cruelty to Animals. There might not be any laws for children, but there were some to protect animals. She said that, as a human being, Mary Ellen was a member of the animal kingdom. Thus, the child had the same rights as a cat or a dog to be protected against cruel treatment.

Gerry, an attorney, agreed with the worker's view. He took her argument to court and won. The judge ordered that Mary Ellen be removed from the home and sent to safety.

After the trial, Gerry founded the New York Society for the Prevention of Cruelty to Children. Word of the organization quickly spread and similar societies took shape across the country in the next years. They all worked to better the lives of children in every way possible. They filed complaints against abusive parents and employers. They worked with the authorities in investigating cases. They sought laws to protect the young and to provide financial help for those in need.

Thanks to the societies and to the work of many other people, all the states eventually enacted laws making it a crime to abuse a child.

STATE LAWS

The laws that the states have passed vary greatly. But there are some things that can be said about them in general.

For instance, if a child is injured and recovers, the parent will likely be charged with assault and battery. Should the child die, the charge may range from manslaughter to first-degree murder. In many states, a person found guilty of injuring a child can be imprisoned for up to a year and fined $1,000 or more.

Once the laws were passed, methods for handling abuse cases began to take shape. As do the laws, these methods today vary across the country, but have some things in common.

Reports of abuse are investigated as quickly as possible. The child is removed from the home if badly hurt, or if there is the danger that he or she will be injured in the future. The child is then placed in someone's care—either at a public facility or in a foster home—while the courts decide what should be done. Sometimes the parents are punished. Sometimes they're sent to programs meant to help them. The child is usually returned home when it is thought safe to do so.

THE PUBLIC AWAKENS

Though the societies and others did excellent work in the late nineteenth century and again in our century, there was as yet no great public outcry against abuse. Most Americans didn't see the problems clearly or didn't know much about it. Busy with their own lives, they were content to let a few dedicated people take care of it.

Then, in the 1960s, word began to reach the public that child abuse was a growing menace. Those men and women who had been left to deal with it—the doctors, nurses, social workers, and police—said that more and more children were being beaten, injured, and killed each year. Drs. Kempe and Helfer wrote *The Battered Child*. A book came from Dr. Fontana. It was called *Somewhere a Child Is Crying*.

At the same time, some shocking cases of abuse began to make headlines. One of the most appalling was that of three-year-old Roxanne Felumero.

In 1969, New York City authorities removed Roxanne from her home and sent her parents to court on charges of beating and neglecting her. But the charges could not be proved. The parents were released. Roxanne was returned to them. Two months later, the child's battered and weighted-down body was found in the East River.

A later case that enraged the public just as much, concerned a four-year-old girl in rural Tennessee. Her name was Melisha Gibson.

Her story began in the early 1970s when her mother and stepfather—a man named Ronnie Maddux—were jailed for beating her. Their sentence ran for six months. Melisha, who was just eleven months old at the time, was placed in a foster home. She stayed there until she was four years old when she was returned to her mother and stepfather.

Ronnie Maddux was said to be an alcoholic who was almost always out of a job. One night soon after Melisha's return, he became angry with her for not going to sleep and then wetting the bed. The next day, he decided to tire out the child so that she would sleep that night and not bother him.

Maddux ordered the child to walk continually back and forth between the kitchen and the bedroom. Every time she passed him, he hit her with a stick. At intervals, he made her drink hot sauce. All the while, he refused to give her any water.

This sort of torture continued throughout the day. Then, when Melisha was asleep that night, he woke her up and put her in a cold shower. The child was dead the next morning.

Ronnie Maddux and his wife were brought to trial. Both were charged with first-degree murder. Both received prison sentences of ninety-nine years.

ACTION

Child abuse was finally recognized as a national problem by the 1970s. It was being talked about everywhere—in homes, in the press, on radio, and on television. People realized that most abusive parents were not as cruel as the Felumeros and Madduxes. But they knew that the problem was serious.

Action was needed.

4
ACTION

Action was needed, and action is what the country was getting. It came from three directions: (1) the states and their local communities, (2) the federal government, and (3) the people themselves.

STATE ACTION

Before the authorities in your hometown can do anything to help a child, they need to know that he or she is being mistreated. Someone has to see or suspect the problem. And then report it to them.

But most people are afraid to make a report. Suppose that you're a neighbor. You may fear that you'll be branded a busybody or that you'll get into a terrible fight with the neighbors. And, since you're reporting a possible crime, you know that you may have to go to court and testify. It's a prospect that can unnerve anybody.

And, not long ago, if your accusations could not be

proved, you were leaving yourself open to being sued by the parents. Perhaps you'd be sued for damaging their name and for interfering with their right to raise their children as they saw fit.

Or suppose that you're a doctor. You may be just as fearful. You may be suspicious but find it impossible to say whether the injuries came from a beating or an accident. It can also be hard not to believe a weeping mother who insists that her little boy fell down the stairs. And it's hard to think about spending hours or days in court when your other patients need you. And there was a time when you, too, could be sued if you were wrong.

These are all very real worries. They have kept many people—not only neighbors and doctors but also nurses, social workers, and teachers—from reporting suspected trouble. Without these reports, thousands of cases have never come to the attention of the authorities over the years.

In the 1960s, all fifty states recognized this problem. They tried to do something about it by passing new laws.

Depending on the state, the new laws either required or encouraged doctors to report all known and suspected cases of abuse and neglect to the local authorities. The authorities were then to investigate the reports as soon as possible, usually within twenty-four hours.

Even before the passage of these laws, the authorities always tried to get to a case quickly. Fast action is the best way to save the child from additional harm. Also, the more time that passes after an incident, the harder it becomes to learn whether there was abuse. Cuts and bruises heal. Memories blur as to what actually happened. The parents have a better chance to work up a strong alibi.

At the present time, practically all of the states *require* a doctor to make a report. The remaining ones—only a few, as this is being written—encourage the doctor to do so. If the doctor lives in a state that requires a report, he or she can be fined or jailed for deliberately keeping quiet.

36

Practically every state, however, protects the doctor from being sued by the parents, granting immunity from such suits.

There is a reason why the laws call for reports from a doctor and not from other people. Doctors often see the victims first, and they're certainly qualified to determine whether the injuries were caused by a beating or an accident. But now many states are pushing for stronger measures. They want to require reports from *everyone*—neighbors, nurses, teachers, clergymen, social workers, attorneys, and policemen.

So far, the reporting laws are proving helpful. The state of Virginia, for instance, saw the number of its reports go up 61 percent during 1974. In New Jersey, the number of reports rose 119 percent between 1973 and 1975. Other states have reported similar jumps.

This has all been encouraging progress. But the reporting problem is still far from being solved. The authorities are sure that the public is still fearfully keeping quiet about thousands of cases.

COMMUNITY ACTION

Talk about community action must begin with the fact that it's a crime to abuse a child.

But almost all experts in child care are against handling the parent as a criminal. Their chief concern is the protection of the child against future harm. But the aim of criminal handling is punishment—and punishment does nothing to safeguard the child. After all has been said and done—even after there's been a jail term—the parent is likely to go right back to beating the youngster again. What happened to Melisha Maddux is a tragic case in point.

On top of this, there is the growing understanding that most abusive parents are not criminals in the first place. Nor are most of them psychotic. Rather, most are the kinds of people we talked about in chapter 2—ordinary people with personal problems beyond their control. Treating them as criminals does nothing to cure the problems that triggered the beatings. Unless there is a cure, the beatings will continue.

Finally, there is the growing belief that it does more harm than good to take most children out of their homes for long periods, as so often happens now while the courts are deciding what should be done about a case.

Some children must be removed—yes, even permanently—for their own protection. They are the Melisha Madduxes and Roxanne Felumeros of this world. But, for the majority of families, the taking away is seen as too emotionally upsetting for everyone. Hardest hit of all is the child. To add to the hurt of the beatings, the child suddenly finds himself or herself in strange and bewildering surroundings—perhaps a public child-care facility, perhaps a foster home.

If the child goes to a foster home, he or she is likely to stay there for a long time. Studies show that the average stay in many areas is more than three years. During that time, the youngster may come to love the foster parents. Then the child suffers the upset of being torn from them and sent back home.

All these understandings are causing more and more local areas—counties and cities—to try doing things a new way with most families.

THE NEW APPROACH

This new approach looks on abuse as a disease and says that it should be treated as such. The treatment consists of three parts: (1) helping the parent to get rid of the problems that cause the abuse, (2) preventing future trouble, and (3) keeping the family together while things are being solved, or getting everyone back together again as soon as possible.

In general, under the new approach, only the worst offending and most dangerous parents are sent to court for criminal action. All others go to trained workers for help. As we'll see in a moment, a wide variety of workers may be used. In some communities, the court watches over their work and may even supervise them. But it takes no criminal action unless the parents can't or—as sometimes happens—won't be helped. Efforts may also be made to help parents who must go to court in the first place or who must be sent there later.

An example of how the new approach works is seen in Nashville, Tennessee, where child abuse cases are handled by an experimental program called the Comprehensive Emergency Services.

One night, an eleven-year-old boy was picked up by police while he was wandering the streets in search of a place to sleep. He was turned over to a Service worker, who learned that his mother and father were alcoholics. The worker met with the parents and talked them into attending a clinic that could help them overcome their problem. They were also given the names of several people—all recovered alcoholics—whom they could call for help anytime they found themselves slipping toward another drinking bout.

The boy had to be placed in a foster home for a while. But an arrangement was made to reunite him with his parents as soon as possible. For every session that the parents attended at the clinic, the boy was allowed to come home for a weekend. Soon, the family was back together again.

Much emphasis is being put on the new approach in Denver, where Dr. Kempe works at the University of Colorado School of Medicine. In the early 1970s, the National Center for the Prevention and Treatment of Child Abuse and Neglect was formed at Denver. Dr. Kempe was named as its director.

The center is fighting abuse with a number of programs.

First, it has formed what are known as child protection teams. Their main job is to look at new abuse cases in the city and suggest the best ways of handling them and helping the parents overcome the causes of the trouble. They also keep track of how previously reported cases are progressing.

On the teams are pediatricians, psychiatrists, social and welfare workers, nurses, policemen, and educators. Also helping are representatives from local churches and minority groups.

Another center program uses what are known as parent aides. These are interested and dedicated citizens who work with the parents in all ways possible to prevent future abuse. Under the supervision of a professional social worker, they visit the homes to see how things are going. They're ready to take telephone calls at any time of the day or night when stress is high and there's the chance of a beating. They'll then talk with the parents—or go to visit them immediately —in an effort to help them "cool down" and get past the danger point.

The aides are important in another way. They're always friendly and sympathetic. They try to show that they really like the parents. This ties in with a point made in chapter 2 —that many abusive parents lash out because they were deprived of love as children. The aides in a sense try to provide that needed love. In a way, they become parents to the parents. Tensions are eased and many a beating is avoided through this show of care.

Still another center program is called Families Anonymous. This is an organization made up of abusive parents. They meet regularly to talk about their problems and to help each other solve them.

As a result of these programs—and some started by the local police and courts—Denver posted a banner year in 1975. For the first time in five years, the city didn't suffer a single death from child abuse.

INNOVATIVE PROGRAMS

Innovative programs have been launched in other communities across the country. For instance, ever since little Roxanne Felumero's death, New York City has been strongly committed to the new approach.

The city has set up a system for investigating all reports of abuse within twenty-four hours. The cases are then handled by a special court—the family court. Unless absolutely necessary, the court doesn't treat the cases as criminal matters. Rather, the parents are sent to counseling sessions that will help them overcome their abuse problem.

In New York and several other cities, some of the help is given at what are known as residential treatment centers. These are homelike places where a number of especially troubled parents can live together with their children while rebuilding their lives. Some of the centers accept only the mothers and the children. Others admit both parents. Some are supported by taxes, and some by private funds.

One of the best-known centers is Odyssey Institute in New York City. The parents and children may remain in most centers for just a few weeks or months, but they may stay at Odyssey Institute for up to three years.

Thanks to Dr. Fontana's pioneering work at New York's Foundling Hospital, the city has a program of parent aides. Like the aides in Denver, they're ready to help the parents at any time.

Many of the aides work with very young mothers. Their help can be quite varied. It may range from giving tips about child care to showing someone how to cook, shop, or sew. In all, the aides serve as good models for the young mothers to copy in growing up and meeting the challenges of parenthood.

The aides have done much to prevent abuse. The same can be said of yet some other New York City workers—the "emergency homemakers." They move into the home and do anything—from cooking and dusting to talking—that will help ease tensions when things are bad and the children are in danger. Emergency homemakers can also be found in Chicago, Atlanta, and Buffalo.

Hartford, Connecticut, works to prevent future trouble by sponsoring a program of outings and trips for families with abuse problems. Prevention is also behind the "crisis nurseries" found in such cities as Denver and Atlanta. Parents may leave their children at the nurseries for safekeeping during danger periods.

On the West Coast, the University of California at Los Angeles opened a string of store-front clinics in 1976. They're for all parents who want to solve their abuse problems or need a place where they can "cool down" when trouble is about to explode.

A number of hospitals across the country have started long-range prevention programs. Nurses and other workers in maternity wards are being taught to look for signs of future abuse in new mothers. A mother who doesn't want to see her newborn infant; a mother who is angry at the birth of a handicapped child; a mother who is overly worried about financial problems—all these may be women who are headed for terrible trouble. Once they've been sighted, the hospital can give them social help.

Many school districts have launched programs to help teachers detect the early signs of abuse and neglect in their students so that help can be given.

HOTLINES

In addition to their other programs, many areas have installed telephone "hotlines." These are numbers that troubled parents may call when they decide that they must stop beating their children and find help. Battered and neglected children may use the hotlines, as may people who wish to report cases of abuse. The lines are manned by trained workers who talk calmly with the callers and can give sound advice on where help can be had.

If there is a hotline in your area, your local operator would be able to give it to you in case you ever need it. There is also a national hotline. It's maintained by the Parents Anonymous Association and may be called toll-free from anywhere in the continental United States. The number is 800-421-0353.

FEDERAL ACTION

For years now, there have been federal laws pertaining to children. They've primarily been laws to protect the young against unfair labor practices and to provide financial help when a child is in need.

An example of how children have been protected by federal law is seen in the Social Security Act, which Congress passed in 1935. Among its other purposes, the act set up funds that, in its words, were to be used for "the protection and care of homeless, dependent, and neglected children and children in danger of becoming delinquent."

In 1962, further protections went into the act. They required the states to make welfare services and programs available to all children when needed. Federal funds were set aside to help the states with this work. Most of the money was spent for families on welfare and for children living in foster homes.

Although willing to help young workers and the needy, Congress had always been unwilling to take steps against abuse by parents. Remember how the legislators of the eighteenth and nineteenth centuries had felt about British common law and about any measure that might interfere with parental rights? A similar reluctance was felt in the twentieth century. By now, all the states had passed laws making it a crime for a parent to abuse a child. As a result, federal legislators had come to think of abuse as a matter best left to the states. They had no desire to interfere.

This attitude, however, was beginning to change by 1962 when the additions were made to the Social Security Act. The first news of abuse as a growing problem was out. Along with the other money set aside for children, Congress authorized some funds to help the states to research in abuse and neglect.

All the reluctance of old finally collapsed as the 1970s approached. Abuse was recognized as a national evil, and it was obvious that it was still growing. The public wanted action. The states were passing their reporting laws. The federal legislators decided to lend a hand.

They introduced a number of bills in Congress. One came from fifteen senators, among them future Vice-President Walter Mondale of Minnesota. Congress studied and revised the bill during 1973 and then enacted it as law on January 31, 1974.

The new law was called the Child Abuse Prevention and Treatment Act. Its purpose was very simple: to help the states and local communities better identify, prevent, and treat abuse and neglect. The help was to come in two ways.

First, the act established the National Center on Child Abuse and Neglect. The center was made a part of the Department of Health, Education, and Welfare. To it went the job of studying all aspects of abuse and neglect. Its findings were to be given to any public agency, private group, school, hospital, or individual working on the problem.

The center was also to develop training materials that could help the states and local areas in starting and running abuse prevention programs. It was to set up teams of technical workers who could go out and give advice on programs. Finally, there was to be an advisory board that would coordinate all federal work in abuse and neglect.

Second, the act made funds available to finance new programs and studies that the states and local communities wanted to try. Set aside for this work was $85 million. The act was to last for a four-year period—from January 1974 to January 1978.

In those four years, the funds were put to a variety of uses. For example, they financed the start of Nashville's Comprehensive Services Program that was mentioned earlier. They went to a special treatment center at Children's Hospital in Boston. The center provides treatment and care for battered children after they've been released from the hospital. A nearby day-care center for abusive parents was also helped by the funds.

At the opposite end of the country, the funds went to the Los Angeles Children's Hospital for a five-year research project. The project hopes to learn how local social service agencies, health departments, and volunteer workers can best work together in treating abuse problems in large urban areas. Out of the study may come a treatment program that can be used as a model for cities everywhere to follow.

In all, more than sixty programs and research projects received the funds. The states were also granted the funds for other work in abuse and neglect.

The act's four-year life came to an end in early 1978. Congress then extended it for another two years and provided it with more money.

In this chapter, we've seen the states, their local communities, and the federal government at work. But the people, remember, have also been busy.

What have they been doing?

5
HELPING HANDS

People have extended a helping hand by forming organizations to fight abuse. Some of these organizations are national in scope. Others work at the state or local level. Though many have come into being within just the past few years to meet the growing threat of abuse, quite a few have been in operation for a long while.

Let's begin by looking at the older ones.

The oldest of all are the Societies for the Prevention of Cruelty to Children. They began to take shape right after Eldridge T. Gerry went to court for Mary Ellen Wilson in the early 1870s. Since then, they've been working to safeguard and better the lives of children in all ways possible—from the filing of complaints against abusive parents to the seeking of stronger protective laws. Today, the Societies are to be found in communities all across the country.

THE AMERICAN HUMANE ASSOCIATION

Another organization with many years of experience behind it is the American Humane Association (AHA). It marked its one-hundredth birthday in 1977. Working on a national scale, the AHA seeks to protect both children and animals.

The work with children is handled by the Child Protection Division, which is headquartered at Englewood, Colorado. Its jobs are many. One of the most important is to assist communities everywhere in developing new programs for protection or in improving the ones already in existence.

The Division carries out research in all aspects of child abuse, neglect, and exploitation. It also prepares instructional materials for school classes studying social service work. Staff members are often asked to lead special classes and workshops for public and private child-care groups. Finally, the Division keeps a close eye on state laws concerning young people and makes suggestions for needed changes.

THE CWLA

Yet another long-time organization is the Child Welfare League of America (CWLA), which was founded early in this century. With its main offices in New York City, the CWLA is an association of child welfare agencies in the United States and Canada. Its basic aim is the constant improvement of the welfare work being done for the needy, abused, and neglected children in the two countries.

As does the AHA, the League works in a variety of ways. It sets high standards for welfare agencies to follow in their work. It consults with the agencies to help them do a better job. It researches all areas of child care. It publishes a wide range of materials for professional welfare workers and any interested citizen. The materials run from pamphlets to textbooks.

But, now, what of the organizations that have come into being to meet the present threat of abuse? Most of them began at the local level. From there, some have grown until they can be found at work all across the country. All were started by troubled citizens who saw that abuse had become a wildfire and who wanted to do something to put it out.

We can get a good idea of what all these groups are doing by looking at two of the most interesting and best known. The first of the two got its start in southern California. Its name: Parents Anonymous.

PARENTS ANONYMOUS

The young woman is known as Jolly K. Her parents abused her when she was young and she spent much of her childhood in foster homes and institutions—thirty-seven in all. Then, when she was grown and married, she began to beat her own children. A nightmare was repeating itself.

Jolly K. couldn't stand the pain and sorrow that she was causing. She looked about for some program that could help her to stop. But there were none to be found. At last, she took her problem to therapist Leonard Lieber, her social worker.

Lieber told the young mother that she was not alone. There were many abusive parents who were just as desperately searching for help as she. He had a suggestion. Why didn't she start a program for them all? She could then help herself by helping them.

Jolly K. nodded, liking the suggestion. The result was Parents Anonymous, which she formed in 1970. Lieber helped her to get it started.

Parents Anonymous is a self-help organization. The idea behind it is based on the approach that Alcoholics Anonymous has long used in helping people who drink too much.

What happens is this: The members get together regularly, usually once a week. They speak openly and honestly to each other about their problem and about the harm their actions have done. Then they try to help each other change their ways and rebuild their lives so that abuse becomes a thing of the past.

To avoid any embarrassment, the members need only use their first names at the meetings. Some choose to go by their full names. Though most members join in the talk, no one is forced to do so. A member may just sit and listen if he or she wishes.

A professional counselor—someone from the social service or mental health fields—usually attends the meetings and gives assistance when needed. The meetings are open not only to parents who have already abused their children but also to all who feel in danger of doing so at some time in the future.

The members exchange telephone numbers so that they can quickly get in touch with each other in case there's trouble between meetings. To get help, members have only to dial when they feel themselves boiling over and becoming a danger to their children.

The benefits to be had from the meetings are many. The talk gives them a way to let off steam. Reduced are all those tensions that would have once exploded in a beating. The help can be of a very practical nature because it comes from the personal experience of the other parents. For instance, one young mother was always scolding and criticizing her six-year-old son. As a result, the child was timid and overly nervous. Several members suggested that she start to change things by making a point of saying something nice to the boy when next he came into a room.

At first, the mother couldn't think of anything to say. Then one morning she complimented him for doing a good job of keeping his room clean. She got a surprised and delighted smile in return. She told the members that she almost cried when she saw it. The young woman had never thought that anything she said could make another person happy.

Parents Anonymous began in 1970 with just one chapter. It then grew steadily until there are now more than eight hundred chapters in the United States and several in foreign countries. It also served as the inspiration for starting Families Anonymous, the program that was mentioned in chapter 4 and that plays such an important role in Dr. Kempe's center at Denver.

Jolly K. has a great ambition for Parents Anonymous. She wants to see it open a chapter in every American community so that its help will be within easy reach of all abusive parents.

CALM

Parents Anonymous is fighting abuse in one way. Let's turn now to an organization that's working in another way. It's called Child Abuse Listening Mediation, but is far better known simply by its initials—CALM.

In 1970, a nineteen-year-old father in Santa Barbara, California, flew into a rage when his tiny son would not stop crying. The father lashed out with his fists. Moments later, the boy was dead. It was a tragedy that shocked and angered the entire city. The child was just eight weeks old.

Just as horrified as everyone else was Claire Miles, a nurse and the mother of four children. But there was pity mixed in with her feelings, especially after she heard of what had happened when a social worker visited the father in jail.

The social worker had been sympathetic and had gently asked why he had struck his son. Though silent and withdrawn since his arrest, the father responded quickly to this show of kindness. He broke down and sobbed that he had felt suffocated by all his responsibilities and daily problems —so suffocated that he had finally given in to a blind fury.

Mrs. Miles realized that he was not a cruel killer, but an ordinary young man who had been overwhelmed by life. She

53

felt that he might never have killed his son had there been a sympathetic person to listen to his troubles all along. There must be many other parents as dangerously upset as he. She suddenly wanted to do something to help them avoid his tragedy.

The "something" that she did turned out to be CALM. It is an organization that is staffed chiefly by volunteer workers—interested and dedicated people from throughout the community. As its initials indicate, its prime purpose is to quiet upset parents by sympathetically listening to them and helping them before harm is done. To do this job, CALM today sponsors a number of programs.

CALM's most basic program is its telephone hotline. Troubled parents may dial it at any time. They'll get an answer both day and night from a volunteer at the other end of the line who will listen and talk for as long as it takes to help them.

The hotline number is well known throughout the Santa Barbara area. It's advertised in the local newspapers and thumbtacked to the bulletin boards in schools, churches, public buildings, and business offices. Many parents, sensing that they may be headed for trouble, have jotted it down and now carry it in their wallets or purses so that it's always right at hand. All calls are kept confidential.

By itself, the hotline has prevented many beatings. But the volunteers are prepared to do more than just listen and talk. They're able to advise a caller of where to turn for further help. Some callers can be helped by the local social services agencies. Some are advised to visit CALM's professional counselors.

The professional counselors are local psychiatrists and psychologists who have agreed to treat callers for fees that, if necessary, will be less than those charged regular patients. Together, a counselor and, say, a young mother on a tight budget will work out a fee that she can afford. One psychologist agreed to a fee of just seventy-five cents for each counseling session.

Parents are not the only ones to use the hotline. Troubled neighbors have called to report beatings that they know about or suspect. Even battered children have dialed for help.

CALM also has a program of parent aides. They do everything they can to help the distressed parent stay clear of trouble—everything from visiting the home daily to taking the children away on outings when things are especially bad. In brief, they do all possible to be a good friend who understands and is sympathetic.

Finally, CALM conducts a public information program on abuse. CALM volunteers often appear as speakers at meetings of civic and private clubs. They also go into the schools to talk with the students and explain what the young people can do to keep abuse out of their homes when they one day become parents.

MORE PEOPLE AT WORK

Thus far, we've talked about five organizations. They were chosen because they were among the first to be formed, either years ago or more recently as the threat of abuse grew. But there are many other groups working alongside them. For example:

1. More and more community hotlines are opening up as the years go by. In 1973, there were approximately sixty hotlines in the country. It's now estimated that the number is well above the one hundred mark.

2. In Chicago, the National Committee for Prevention of Child Abuse is conducting a nationwide program to alert the country to the dangerous spread of abuse.

3. The SCAN service provides volunteers to work as

parent aides in the counties of Arkansas. SCAN stands for Suspected Child Abuse and Neglect.

4. The Panel for Family Living in Tacoma, Washington, is made up of volunteers who conduct classes in therapy and child raising for troubled parents. The volunteers also serve as parent aides.

5. Family Focus in Birmingham, Michigan, operates a hotline and holds classes to help parents better understand their children and the needs of the young.

If you were to count up all the organizations in the country, you'd find that thousands of thoughtful and concerned Americans are working to halt the spread of abuse. Now let's suppose that you'd like to join them. As a young person, what can you do to place your helping hand alongside their helping hands?

6
YOUR
HELPING HAND

When the time comes, of course, you'll be able to join one of the organizations. But this is something for the future. In the meantime, there are some things that you very definitely can do. There is, first, something that you can do among your friends. And then some things that you can do at home *if there is abuse there.*

What you can do is alert all your friends to the problem of abuse, and show them how dangerous it is. Why not ask that it be made a topic for discussion or study in your current events or social studies class at school? Or that your church group, neighborhood club, or Scout troop set aside some time to talk about it?

Then, why not bring in some materials that can be used in the discussion? There's much to be found on the subject— in magazines, in the daily papers, and in books at the public library. To help you get started, there's a section entitled "A Selected Reading List" at the end of this book.

And why not ask an expert in the field of child protection to talk to your group or class? A police juvenile officer would be a good choice. So would someone from your local social service or welfare agencies. And, of course, someone from a local hotline or a group such as CALM.

All your work can bring some fine results. The information may help a friend who, though you've never guessed it, has long been abused at home. A future doctor or nurse may one day be working especially with battered children because of an interest that you sparked. And you may be starting other of your friends on the way to becoming tomorrow's volunteer workers with abusive parents.

IF THERE'S ABUSE AT HOME

What can you do to help solve the problem if abuse is a part of life in your home? If your little brother or sister is being beaten? Or if you yourself are the victim?

I asked these questions of a psychologist. She replied that, sadly, there is really nothing that a very small and defenseless child can do. But an older child, she added, need not be helpless. She had five suggestions for the older child.

Let me pass them on to you.

Dangerous "When's"

It may be painful to do so, but start by looking at past beatings. See if you can find definite times *when* they've happened. For instance, have there been beatings when your mother has had a headache? Or when Dad has come home complaining that "my stomach is killing me"? Or when your parents have had a fight?

Should you sight some "when's," then watch out for them in the future. Anytime one crops up, try to do what you can to keep your parents from getting too tense. Perhaps it will help if you take over some of the housework and cooking from Mother. Or take your little brother or sister out for a walk or a romp in the park. You may be giving your parents just the chance they need to simmer down and keep their fists from clenching.

Annoying Habits

As you review the past, also give yourself a check. Do you have some habit that annoys your parents? If so, try your best to get rid of it. Some funny little habit may not really bother your parents when they're feeling all right. But when there's tension, anything can cause trouble—a blaring radio, a messy room, clothes strewn about, or a skateboard always carelessly left underfoot.

Keep Yourself under Control

If you've been beaten before, it's natural to be afraid of another beating when life goes wrong in the house. But try to keep this fear under control so that you don't accidentally do something that worsens matters and actually brings on a new beating. My psychologist friend tells of what fear did to a patient of hers when he was a boy.

"He'd know that things were wrong with his parents and he'd be afraid, all jittery inside. Then—almost as if he had no control over it—he'd do something foolish. He wouldn't want to, but he still would. . . . He'd knock something over and break it. . . . He'd disobey. . . . He'd talk back. . . . He'd burst out crying. . . . And, as he says, 'That would do it. I'd be in for trouble'."

And so, as difficult as it may be, it is always wise to keep a firm grip on your fear. The same goes for your pride and anger.

Let's say that you're arguing at the dinner table because you want to stay out past midnight on a date. Your dad says that you must be home by ten and he's starting to lose control. Don't let your pride or anger keep you from pulling back and trying again later when he's calmed down. Or don't let him keep you from agreeing to a compromise time—say, eleven o'clock. Or why not just come home at ten o'clock as he wants?

Your pride may be hurt a little. But, regardless of our age, we all have to pull back at times or make compromises in our dealings with people. Also, a pulling back or a compromise—each so often indicating that you appreciate the other person's point of view—can work wonders. And, of course, either is better than a blowup that sees you hit or thrown against a wall.

Your Brothers and Sisters

As your little brothers and sisters grow older, talk over the above points with them so that they can begin to protect themselves. Speak quietly so that you don't frighten them. Then do your best to help them always avoid trouble.

Reporting Abuse

This fifth and final point is the most difficult one to talk about. It concerns reporting the abuse in your home to the authorities.

Many young people—even those well into their teens—quietly endure beatings and neglect without ever reporting them. The reasons for their silence are many. Some youngsters are afraid the parents will be jailed and the family broken up. Some don't want to see their parents humiliated. Others fear that they themselves will be shamed. And some even fear that the parents will take revenge on them.

These are very reasonable fears. There *are* definite risks in reporting abuse. If the abuse is severe, it *is* possible that your parents will be arrested. It *is* possible that you'll be placed in a foster home for a time.

But these dangers must be weighed against the dangers

of remaining silent. Will you be physically, emotionally, or mentally injured, perhaps for life? Will a little brother or sister be badly hurt?

The answers to these questions may show you how necessary it is to make a report.

Should you decide to seek help, social workers say that it's best not to go to the police. This doesn't mean that the police aren't capable of helping you. They are. The problem is that they will usually investigate your report as if a crime has been committed. The risk is great that your parents will be arrested.

Rather, it's wiser to turn to a public agency that deals with the problems of children. Good choices would be the county probation office, the local social service agency, or a youth protection agency. Many of these agencies work according to the new approach that was described in chapter 2. And so they'll likely try to handle your report at what's called the family level.

This means that they'll get in touch with your parents and talk with them. They may be able to straighten things out by warning them of what lies ahead if the abuse continues. They may be able to get your parents to enter a counseling program—or an organization such as Parents Anonymous—that will help put an end to the problems that caused the abuse.

All this may be done without calling in the police and running the risk of an arrest. The agencies will usually get in touch with the police only if the abuse is so bad that your health or life is threatened. Of course, the police will have to be called if your parents refuse help and go on hurting you.

Before you go to the outside for help, you may want to see if something can be done inside the family. Is there a trusted relative or family friend you can turn to? If either can talk on your behalf, they may help your parents see the harm they're doing and the sorrow they're causing.

But there's a risk involved here that you should know about. How will your parents act when they learn that a relative or a friend has found out how they treat you? As you hope, will they be jolted into wanting to change their ways? Or will they be so angry that there will be another beating? Think things over carefully before you make a move.

Probably the best way to start is to call the hotline in your area. Explain your problem to the worker who answers. The worker will listen sympathetically and will tell you what you should do next and where it's wisest to go for help. He or she may be able to make the report for you. And the worker may be able to keep your name out of things, at least for a while.

If your hometown is without a hotline, then you can turn to the national hotline that was mentioned in chapter 4. The person who answers will likely be able to tell you where to find help in your own area.

The decision to report abuse in your home is a difficult one. I hope that what we've talked about here will be of help if ever you have to make that decision. And I hope that the other four points will help in safeguarding you and your brothers and sisters against abuse.

We've now come to the end of the chapters on battered and neglected children. It's time to turn to another problem.

7
SEXUALLY
ABUSED
CHILDREN

Do you remember eleven-year-old Bobby in chapter 1? He's the boy who lived with his aunt and was made to take off all his clothes whenever her friends came to visit.

Bobby was called an abused child because of the damage his aunt did to his spirit. Her actions added up to the kind of mistreatment known as sexual abuse. It's an abuse suffered by countless children across the world.

Sexual abuse is also known as molestation, which means "to make indecent advances toward someone." Both young children and teen-agers can be its victims. It takes many forms.

For instance, a man approaches a child or a group of children playing on the sidewalk or in a park. He wears an overcoat. He opens it, shows them that he is nude, and then hurries away after a moment or two.

Or a car draws up alongside a small boy or girl walking home from school. The man at the wheel lures the child into the car with an offer of candy or ice cream. Sometimes he says that he's a friend of the family and wants to give the youngster a lift home. The child is then driven away and made to perform some sexual act with him.

Or—as happened in northern California recently—a teen-age girl disappears while hitchhiking. Last seen by friends as she was trying to thumb her way across town to a record store, she was found two weeks later in a remote wooded area. She had been raped and then strangled.

Molestations such as these are one-time occurrences. But, as in Bobby's case, the victims can also be accosted again and again over a period of time. In Ohio recently, an elderly man was arrested for pawing several neighborhood tots whom he was always inviting in for milk and cookies. He told them that it was all a "game" and asked them to keep it a secret from their parents. Not old enough to know better, the children obeyed. Only after several weeks did one little girl accidentally let the secret slip out.

On the West Coast, a woman teacher in a junior high school was arrested after two girls accused her of taking them to her apartment several times for sexual acts. The incidents had taken place over a period of eighteen months.

One case of continuing abuse that shocked the entire nation some months ago took place in the Boston area. Arrested were ten men, among them a psychiatrist, a psychologist, and two teachers. They had struck up friendships with a number of boys ranging in age from nine to thirteen. They had then used the boys for homosexual acts.

The boys were each paid from five dollars to fifty dollars every time they took part. In the apartment of one of the men, police found photographs of more than eighty nude boys.

Modern medicine looks on the sexual abuse of children as the result of a mental or emotional sickness in some adults. Like most sicknesses, it knows neither geographical nor time boundaries and has been in all parts of the world for centuries. It was known in ancient Greece and Rome, just as it is known in every country today. Sexual abuse has long been considered one of the most detestable of crimes. It shocks the moral standards of all countries. Both men and women can be abusers, but the man is far more often the offender.

No one knows for certain how many children are accosted here in the United States. There are no complete figures on the number of sexual abuses that occur each year. And, as happens with child beatings, most cases go unreported.

But we do have some figures. They indicate that molestation is widespread and may equal or even surpass child beating as a problem. The National Center on Child Abuse and Neglect, for instance, estimates that at least 100,000 young Americans suffer some kind of sexual abuse each year. Some experts say that this figure is far too low. They feel that it should be up over the quarter-million mark.

We may have no real idea of how many victims there are, but we have learned a number of other facts about sexual abuse in recent years. They have come to light as hospitals and child-care workers have studied the whole problem of child abuse.

SOME FACTS

First, it's long been believed that girls are more often sexually abused than boys. Now we have learned just how much more. Studies show that girls are the victims ten times more often.

We've also learned that the average age of the victim is eleven years. But children far, far younger have been accosted. Some have been just a few months old.

One study has shattered a belief long held by people everywhere—that children are most often sexually abused by weird strangers who lurk in parks or drive up in cars. In 1967, a study by the American Humane Association found the *exact opposite* to be true.

The AHA learned that only one-quarter of all sexual abuse is committed by strangers. A scant 2 percent takes place in cars. Five percent takes place in abandoned buildings.

But, in a full 75 percent of all cases, the victim knows the assailant—as was true in the cases of the elderly man in Ohio, the teacher on the West Coast, and the ten men in Boston.

Further, in about 34 percent of all cases, the abuse takes place in the victim's home. Here, the victim is usually a girl. The assailant is not someone who breaks into the house. Rather, he's a relative—perhaps her uncle, brother, stepfather, or grandfather—more often her father.

This type of abuse, called incest, can affect the victim and the family in especially terrible ways. It will be the subject of chapter 9.

THE SILENT CRIME

As are child beating and neglect, sexual abuse is a crime in all states. Depending on the state and the act involved, it may be either a misdemeanor or a felony offense. Some acts may earn the offender a fine and several months in jail. Rape of a child can put someone in prison for fifty years or more. In many areas, efforts are made to rehabilitate the offender through counseling or psychiatric care.

Sexual abuse, beatings, and neglect, all share the same problem. As was said a few paragraphs ago, it is a crime that goes unreported too much of the time—so often, in fact, that some authorities call it the silent crime.

There are two understandable reasons for this silence. Both are fears. The first belongs to the child. Fear has caused some victims to carry the secret around inside themselves for years until they could stand it no longer and had to tell their parents. Others have never spoken up.

70

THE CHILD'S FEARS

I've talked about this fear with a social worker who deals with sexual abuse cases. She says that it can take "many forms."

For instance: "I worked with one child who had been pawed in a movie theater. She was afraid to say anything because she thought the man would find her and hurt her for telling on him. . . . Another had been grabbed by a man while she was playing in a park. She got away without harm and then kept quiet for days because her mother had always told her not to play there."

The worker goes on: "There can also be a strong sense of guilt mixed in the fear. I've seen many children who've felt that they did something wrong by letting the assailant touch them. They may have been too little to fight back. Or too scared. But they still felt that somehow they were to blame for taking part. They were sure that Mother and Dad and everyone would say that they had been bad. . . .

"The feeling of guilt can be particularly strong in children who take candy before or after the assault. Young as they may be, they can feel that they were paid for doing what they did and so are to blame."

Some children, she adds, are too embarrassed to talk. Some feel dirty and hope the feeling will go away if they keep quiet and try not to think about it. "Some older children are afraid they'll be accused of having invited the attack. Girls who are old enough to flirt can be especially afraid of this."

PARENTAL FEARS

The second fear comes from the parents. It, too, can take many forms, says the worker. She explains:

"It can be terribly difficult for the parents to go to the

police. They know that an officer is going to have to question the child. That can be an awful experience. It can make the child twice as upset as she already is. I've talked to parents who are afraid that it can scar a child emotionally for life."

There's another worry. "Maybe the incident wasn't a very serious one or maybe the child is too young to understand what happened. The parents say, 'Okay, she'll probably forget about it in a while. But not if we call the police. . . .' "

And still other worries: Some parents fear that any report of the incident will get around the neighborhood or even into the newspapers and embarrass the child and the family. If the assailant is someone known to the child and the family, the parents may not want to have trouble with *his* family or cause them embarrassment. Often, the father will go to the assailant, tell him to stay away, and then drop the matter and hope for the best. (*Note:* There should be no worries about newspaper reports. Virtually every newspaper protects minors by not printing their names.)

All authorities, including the police, agree that the investigation of a sexual offense can do great emotional harm to the child. Why? To begin, there are the questions that the police must ask. As the social worker says, they can be a terrible ordeal. Some children, already frightened, may become doubly frightened when asked to relive their experience. Younger children may be made afraid by all the fuss over something that they really don't understand. And any child, even though not understanding what happened, can still feel humiliated when being made to describe what someone did to him or her.

Older children may be embarrassed by not knowing the correct names of the body areas touched. Or by having to use baby names for them. Or by having to point them out in the absence of any name at all.

And older children are often embarrassed when their

answers give away the fact that they know more about sex than they're sure their parents will like.

The questions are bad enough, but they're not asked just once. An investigation often starts with only a few—just enough to get the police going after the offender. It's then common to talk with the child again, perhaps in a day or so. The questions are repeated and new ones are asked because the police are now after more detailed information. It will be needed to file charges against the offender should he (or she) be caught. And so the ordeal continues.

Let's suppose that the assailant is caught, charged, and sent to trial. Now the child will have to go to court and give testimony. The child may be able to testify in the privacy of the judge's chambers. This is often done in cases involving young people. But, if the assailant calls for a jury trial, the child will have to appear in open court, with a roomful of strangers watching.

It takes no imagination to see what this entire process can do to a child who may be frightened, embarrassed, or bewildered. And who may all the while be suffering a physical injury inflicted by the assailant. It can turn an experience that is perhaps best forgotten, into a terrible memory that never goes away.

And there's something else. What of the children who feel guilty, cowardly, or sick about the attack? The whole process can intensify these feelings so that they become a part of the children and haunt them perhaps for life.

WHAT'S BEING DONE

Although the authorities all regret the harm that can be done through an investigation, they can't call it off. The assailant must be found so that no one else is harmed. And the police must get all the facts from the child if the assailant is to be given a fair trial.

But the authorities also know that something must be done to protect the child's feelings.

And something is being done.

Many police departments have set up special units to handle sexual abuse cases. The officers are all trained to treat the victims gently and quietly. And it has become common practice to have only women officers work with the victims of rape, regardless of the victim's age. Hospitals, too, are training their staffs to deal more skillfully than ever with sexual abuse victims.

It is also common practice in many communities to have the local social service agency join the police in the investigation. Assigned to help are workers trained in dealing with children.

Something else is being done. For many years now, special "protective service programs" have been at work in several East Coast cities. With specially trained workers, these programs are sponsored by the local Societies for the Prevention of Cruelty to Children and have the full cooperation of the police and other authorities. To them goes the job of handling sexual abuse cases. Here's how each works.

When the report of an offense is received, it goes from the police to a protective service worker of the same sex as the victim. The worker immediately talks with the child, often in the family home, and gathers the facts of the case. The worker is always friendly and sympathetic. He or she is careful never to upset or frighten the child or to give the impression that the victim did something wrong.

The worker then puts the facts into a written report for the authorities. If the facts warrant it, the offender will be sought, arrested, and charged.

Once the arrest is made, the worker stays close to the authorities. If necessary, he or she will help them accept a plea of guilty from the offender. Should there be a guilty plea, there will be no trial but only sentencing by the judge. The child won't have to go through the ordeal of testifying.

But let's say that there is to be a trial. Now the worker's job multiplies. He or she will seek to have the case heard in the privacy of the judge's chambers. The worker may try to have the public kept out if the trial must be held in open court. He or she will prepare the child and the parents for the experience of going to court, doing all that is possible to keep them from being frightened by what's to come. Finally, he or she will attend the trial with them and stand by as a close and helpful friend the whole time.

In addition to all this, the worker keeps a constant eye on the child's health. Suppose that the sexual abuse has done some emotional harm. Or perhaps, in spite of the worker's sympathy, the experiences since then have been damaging. He or she will call for special help for the child. Just as important, special help for the parents can be arranged if they, too, are emotionally upset.

In all, the worker serves as a friend and adviser, who helps the family get through a trying experience in a way that will cause them the least suffering, and see them returned as quickly as possible to a normal life.

MORE CAN BE DONE

All these efforts—from the special police units to the protective service programs—have helped many victims of sexual abuse. But child-care workers say that much more must be done if all victims are to be reached.

In their view, at least four things need to be done.

1. All communities should have their child-care workers play the strongest role possible in any investigation and trial. The feeling here is that, though the police may be well trained to work with youngsters, the child-care worker is in a better position to help. The police officers' job is law enforcement; they're the ones best qualified to track down the offender. But the child-care workers' training centers on the family. They're the ones able to help the child and the fam-

ily—the ones best able to provide counseling and other special help.

2. Greater attention must be paid to the parents. They can be as upset and as emotionally damaged as the child—sometimes even more so. Many parents go so far as to think that the youngster has been "ruined for life." All this communicates itself to the child and can do lasting harm. Communities need to develop programs to soothe the parents and help them see things in a sensible light.

3. Strong reporting laws must be passed. All states require that physical child abuse and neglect be reported. But not all the states have the same laws for sexual offenses. In great part, this is because sexual child abuse has been such a "silent crime" that many lawmakers haven't fully realized how widespread a problem it is. Unless the offenses are reported, the community isn't able to help the child and the parents. Nor are the police able to go after the offender and prevent him from harming someone else.

4. Greater attention must be given to helping the offenders overcome the problems that caused the abuse in the first place. Without the effort being made to help them, they'll always be a threat.

8
WHAT YOU CAN DO

As someone who is old enough to read this book, you're old enough to do a good job of protecting yourself against a sexual attack. You're old enough to know and avoid the places where danger may lurk. Old enough to recognize odd behavior in strangers or acquaintances. And old enough to walk away from it.

But the same isn't true of younger children—your little brothers and sisters, the tots in your neighborhood, and the small ones that you may one day be raising. Their innocence makes them especially vulnerable to danger. They need to be protected by anyone who is older.

You can help with this protection. Just put the following suggestions to work. They come from doctors, child-care workers, and the police. They're suggestions that start with what can be done to avoid an attack and then move on to what can be done in the event of trouble.

GUARDING AGAINST TROUBLE

Just what can you do to help your parents safeguard the small children in your family against trouble? What can you do to protect the children you may one day have?

1. *Danger Spots*

There are certain areas in any neighborhood that are obviously danger spots for a child. At the top of the list are alleyways; construction sites after working hours; abandoned buildings; basements and indoor parking areas in apartments; remote or bushy areas in parks; and vacant lots that are screened from the street by fences or billboards.

Children should be taught not to play in these places or in any other dark, deserted, or out-of-the-way spot. Quietly coach them to stick to well-lighted areas where they are known and where there are helpful adults or older children nearby.

It's a good idea to go out with your parents and check the routes that a little brother or sister walks to school, to the store, to music lessons, or to the local playground. If you find some danger spots, then see if you can change the route. Or, always be sure that the youngster is accompanied by an adult or a responsible older child.

Incidentally, the child should always be accompanied if *any* route has to be walked after dark. And no child should ever be allowed to idle or wander about on the way to and from home, no matter how safe the route may seem.

2. *The Child's Schedule*

In addition to knowing the various routes, you should also know the child's schedule. When is little sister due home from school, the library, or her best friend's house? Insist that she come home right at that time. If she doesn't arrive when she should, don't wait too long before you start telephoning to find out where she is. Or go out and begin to look.

It's always wise to know where a child is at all times. A fast search on your part can save the youngster from running into trouble.

3. *Strangers*

What should a child do if approached by a stranger with the offer of candy or a ride? The answer is simple. Without becoming frightened, the youngster should refuse, leave immediately, and head for home. Or, go to a nearby location where she knows the adults—the school grounds, a store, the public library.

The child should also leave if the stranger asks what time it is or wants to chat for a while. Sometimes, a stranger will seek directions from a child. He may actually be lost, but it's best for the youngster to walk away and not take any chances. If the stranger is on foot, the child should never go with him to show him where a place is. If the stranger is in a car, the child should never even come close to it.

Similar cautions need to be taken with adults that the child knows. No youngster should ever walk or ride away with any acquaintance *without first getting permission from his or her parents*. Remember, the studies show that in 75 percent of all sexual cases, the assailant is someone the child knows.

4. *In the House*

A child should never open the front door when the bell rings. That job should be left to adults or teen-agers. If the child is alone for any reason—perhaps Mother has run next door for a moment or is upstairs taking a bath—the bell should be allowed to go right on ringing until the caller gives up and goes away.

The telephone also must be handled with equal care. Suppose that your little brother answers. A strange voice wants to know if Mom or Dad is home. He should never reply, especially if he's alone. Rather, he should ask who is

81

calling. If the caller won't tell him, then he should hang up immediately.

HOW TO TELL THE CHILD

When you start to warn a child of danger, you face a problem. You want to get your ideas across effectively so that they'll be remembered. But you don't want to be scary. So how should you handle things?

First, of course, speak quietly and calmly. Though your subject is serious, there's no need to put a lot of drama into your voice as if you're telling a horror story. You're giving sensible advice. If your manner and tone of voice are sensible, then the advice itself is going to seem all the more sensible and less frightening.

Try not to give the impression that the world is full of sick adults who are looking *especially for children* and just waiting to pounce on them. Rather, be sure to stress that you're talking about the kind of things that all intelligent people do just to be on the safe side, regardless of their age.

You can put this point across more easily if there are older family members present while you're talking. If you have older brothers and sisters, they can lend a hand. Let them say that, as big as they are, they follow similar rules. Or your mother and dad can say the same thing.

In addition, try not to give the impression that the world is full of sick and weird people in the first place. It's wiser to put over the idea that adults who bother children are the exceptions—which is actually the truth of the matter. If you give the wrong impression, the child may begin to suspect and fear *everyone*. That's simply not healthy.

Small children can be very forgetful. The fun of playing or the wonder of new sights can drive all the safeguards from mind at any moment. You're going to need to remind the youngster of them from time to time. Take care that the reminders are just that—reminders and not frightening warnings. Slowly and surely, the advice will take root.

These safeguards should greatly reduce the chances of an attack. But, of course, nothing can altogether wipe out the danger. Let's say that a little sister comes running home after there's been trouble. What can you now do to help her?

First, remain calm. It is important to be careful of the feelings you communicate to her. She may or may not be upset, depending on such things as her age and exactly what has happened.

You want to show your love and concern, but not by going to pieces. If she's upset, your loss of head will worsen matters. If she's not, you may cause her to panic. If she's too young to understand what was done to her, your becoming upset can frighten her; she already knows that something is wrong and now it will seem terrible—all the more so because she doesn't know what it is.

So, quietly check the youngster for physical harm and do all that you can to soothe her. Then visit your family doctor for a further check. The doctor can do much to quiet her if she is upset.

Next, avoid saying or doing anything that will add to any unhealthy feelings that she may have. As you know, an attack may leave a child feeling "dirty," guilty, cowardly, stupid, or even at fault. So don't scold her about forgetting some safeguard or playing in a forbidden spot. Never make a big thing out of the sexual aspects. Don't appear shocked.

Calmness is really your key word throughout. It comes into play as soon as you learn that something is wrong. Then it stays in play as you draw the story of the incident from the youngster. Quietly help her to tell you of everything that happened. Help with the names of the body areas involved or help her to point them out. Get her to describe the assailant as best she can.

If she knows who the assailant is, have her give you his

name. She may be reluctant to do this, perhaps out of fear, more often because so many children feel guilty about "telling on" someone. You'll help matters by not showing any anger at the assailant. Say nothing about wanting the police to catch him so that he can be punished. Rather, let her know that he's ill and that you want him found so that he can be helped.

Even though you may hate the idea, the police should be called. You must do your part to get sexual abuse out of the "silent crime" category. And you must do your part to keep the assailant from getting to and harming other children.

Tell the child what you're going to do and then soothe any fears that she may have. When an officer arrives, stand by to assist in any way that you can. Help the child tell her story. Insist that the officer treat her gently and patiently—as he or she is almost sure to do so anyway, without needing to be told. Try not to let the officer question her for too long a time.

Then, throughout whatever may come later, give the child all your support and love. Finally, when everything is behind her, do all that you can to help her forget the incident and return to a normal and happy life.

9
THE CHILD
AND INCEST

Incest can be defined as sexual acts between two people who are so closely related that the law forbids them to marry.

Just what is meant by "so closely related"? In almost all parts of the world, sex and marriage are forbidden between a father and his daughter, a mother and her son, and a brother and his sister. In many places, the same applies to stepparents and their sons and daughters. So far as other relatives are concerned, however, the ideas on incest vary greatly from society to society.

In some societies, people who are first or second cousins may neither marry nor have sex, but couples who are more distantly related are free to do so. In others, no one may mate with a blood relative, no matter how distant the relationship may be. And in some of those that are made up of tribes or clans, a person must never choose a partner from within his or her own tribe or clan.

Despite the differences in the ideas on incest, most societies agree on one point. They view incest as a moral wrong.

Some aren't particularly worried about it, but many others see it as the worst of moral wrongs, something as terrible as murder or cannibalism. Most societies' feelings about incest come from religious beliefs that date far back to ancient times.

No one knows for certain why early people outlawed sexual acts between closely related couples. A concern about health may have been one reason. Ancient societies may have thought that the couples produced a high percentage of children with birth defects. This health reason could then have been turned into a moral one, with the ancients saying that the couples had done something wrong and that the gods were now punishing them with the defective children.

(*Note*: The belief in a high percentage of defective children still persists today. But recent scientific studies indicate that there may not be too much truth to it. A study made in Japan suggests that breeding by closely related people produces very few harmful physical effects.)

With the feelings against it being so strong in many societies, the punishments for incest have usually been severe. Some ancient communities executed the offenders or banished them to a life of wandering homelessly from place to place. In the England of the seventeenth century, incest was punishable by death. The same held true in Scotland until the late nineteenth century, though the sentences actually given were for life imprisonment.

Today, many countries—our own among them—list incest as an offense that is punishable by a prison term or a fine, or both. In the United States, the penalties are set by state law and vary a great deal across the country. Prison sentences can run from several months to life. Fines can range from a few dollars to $5,000.

While most societies dislike incest between adults, they find it especially hateful when it involves a child. In recent years, Americans have been shocked to learn that incest involving children is a problem here. In terms of our total population, it seems yet to be a relatively small problem. But, in common with all other kinds of child abuse, it is one that is coming more and more to light as time passes.

INCEST IN THE UNITED STATES

Not too long ago, most people thought that there was practically no such thing as incest in the United States. In the mid-1960s, the authorities estimated that there was only one case for every million people.

The following years showed the estimate to be far off the mark. To see just how far, we need only look at the Child Sexual Abuse Treatment Program in San Jose, California.

The program was begun in 1971 to help the victims of all types of sexual abuse. San Jose, which is located near San Francisco, is the major city in a county of more than one million people. Were the authorities and their estimate right, the program could have expected to handle just one incest case a year.

But the fact is that it treated 31 cases in its first year. The number jumped to 145 in 1974. By 1976, the program was handling 170 cases annually. Since then, the yearly total has passed the 500 mark.

The American Humane Association in 1967 found that about 34 percent of all sexual abuse of children takes place in the home and among family members. The National Center on Child Abuse and Neglect estimates that each year at least 100,000 young Americans suffer some kind of sexual abuse, including incest. Other experts say that the total should be over 250,000.

But these are all estimates. We can only say the same thing here that we say about all other abuses: we don't know exactly how many young people are involved. As usual, this is because only a very few cases are ever reported to the authorities. Incest is even more of a "silent crime" than the other sexual abuses.

Fortunately, though, the incest problem is being studied closely by many child-care workers. From them, we're starting to piece together a good picture of what's going on. We've learned, for instance, that incest is not limited to one kind of family or neighborhood. Like the beatings and neglect, it's found among all kinds of people and in neighborhoods from the poorest to the richest.

And we've learned much about the victims.

THE VICTIMS

There are some cases of incest involving boys with their mothers or some other relative. But, in the great majority of cases, the victim is a girl. Her assailant is usually an adult male. He may be an uncle, a cousin, a brother, even a grandfather. Most often, he is the child's father or guardian.

The sexual acts which the victim is made to perform can be many. They often begin with fondling and kissing. Other acts can then follow until, at the end, there is full intercourse.

Studies show that the average age of the sexually abused child is eleven years. Incest, however, often begins when the child is too young to understand what is really happening. Girls four and five years old have been victims, as have infants of just a few months.

The assailant may approach the victim in any of several ways. It's been found that, in about 60 percent of all reported cases, he makes her give in with threats or force. Otherwise, he may coax or lure her into the act. One ten-year-old, for instance, told the authorities that her stepfather said they were going to play a "fun game."

Another child reported her uncle as saying it would be

"a way of showing how much we love each other." Many youngsters have said they were told that "it's a natural thing that everybody does."

The child often innocently gives in because she is pleased by the affection that the adult is showing and doesn't realize what he's planning to do. Often, especially if she's very young, she is simply obeying the adult as she has always been taught to do in other matters.

But what are her feelings when the act is done? Or when she grows old enough to know that something is wrong? Or when somebody tells her the truth?

EMOTIONAL DAMAGE

There can be terrible emotional damage at that moment.

One victim, now a grown woman, tells the story of so many others when she recalls what happened to her. She was twelve at the time. "I was angry with my dad for doing this thing to me. . . . I felt that he wouldn't have made me feel this way if he'd really cared for me. . . . I didn't want to talk to him or have him in the same room with me. I didn't even want to look at him. . . . And I'd always loved and admired him so much. . . . My whole life was changed. . . ."

And there was a feeling of revulsion. "I couldn't stand to have it happen again. Every time I'd think of it, I'd want to throw up."

Other shattering emotions can join the anger and revulsion. They're the same as those felt in other forms of sexual abuse—except that they can hurt more because they have to do with a family member.

Many children feel a deep sense of guilt for having cooperated, even though they were too young at the time to understand what was happening. Those who give in through force or a threat can feel ashamed. When remembering her experience of some years earlier, one young woman wept, "I should have fought back. I wanted to. But I was afraid. And he was so strong . . ."

And some of the children feel to blame for what has happened. This can be especially true of older girls. One thirteen-year-old had on a new dress and was wearing makeup when her father approached her for the first time. She knew that she looked pretty and she wondered if he would have bothered her had she not been so dressed up.

The emotional damage that is done can last a lifetime. For one woman, it lasted as a fear and dislike of men. Others have distrusted all men. Still others have found themselves disgusted by the very idea of sexual love. Many have suffered unhappy marriages. Others have avoided marriage altogether.

There have also been health problems. Severe depression, extreme nervous tension, and migraine headaches have all been seen in former victims. Studies have found that as many as 40 percent of all women who abuse drugs have incest somewhere in their past.

BEHAVIORAL PROBLEMS

As can be expected, the emotions often show their damage in behavioral problems. Some children can release their feelings only by lashing out at the world. Chapin Hall is an Illinois home for disturbed and homeless children. A doctor found that a majority of the girls there had come from sexually abusive families.

The desire to escape from incest is behind some of the behavioral problems. It's well known that many runaways are girls fleeing from sexual abuse.

And it's well known that many of the runaways then turn to prostitution as a livelihood. Minneapolis, Minnesota —along with such cities as Los Angeles and New York—is a mecca for runaways. A recent study showed that 75 percent of the teen-age prostitutes there have incest in their backgrounds.

It is believed that, when they needed money, the runaways turned easily to prostitution because they had come to have such low opinions of themselves as human beings. They seemed to think that all any man wanted from them was sex and that it was all they were good for.

Many victims also seek escape in drugs and alcohol. One therapist in Minnesota has dealt with more than five hundred cases of teen-age drug abuse. He says that about 70 percent of his young patients come from homes where there has been sexual abuse.

THE WHY'S OF INCEST

The reasons why incest occurs can be many. For one twelve-year-old, it began when she came home from a friend's house late one afternoon and found that her parents had been drinking heavily. Her mother had passed out in the living room. Her father followed her into the kitchen, staggered up behind her, and suddenly put his arms around her.

While something as simple as drunkenness can start the trouble, the reasons behind most incest cases are far more complex.

Look at the experience of one family. Things had got so bad that the mother and father no longer talked to each other. The father started to spend more and more time with their eleven-year-old daughter, helping with her homework and watching television with her. He said later that he had no thought of having sexual relations with the child. He was just desperately lonely and wanted her company. But one night when they were alone in the house, the daughter came to give him a good-night kiss. The trouble began at that moment.

In another family, there was, again, no love between husband and wife. The husband turned to their daughter as a way of "hurting" the wife.

Sometimes the victim unwittingly helps to start things. She loves and admires her father. She wants to show her affection and she wants a show of affection in return. And so she'll do what all daughters do at one time or another. She'll sit in his lap, nestle close, and give him a hug.

The normal father responds to this affection in a natural way. The affection he gives back is a father's affection. But the disturbed and lonely father? If the moment is the wrong one for him, he may respond differently and then be unable to control his emotions.

At that moment, both he and his daughter become victims.

ANOTHER SILENT CRIME

As I mentioned earlier, incest is even more of a silent crime than other forms of sexual abuse. Only a scant few cases are reported to the authorities. Los Angeles, with a population in the millions, is one of the largest cities in the country. Yet the Los Angeles Police Department receives just over one hundred reports of sexual abuse by a parent or guardian each year.

The silence begins with the victim. All the reasons here are the same as in other abuses. The child may be too frightened, ashamed, or embarrassed to talk. Or she may somehow still be loyal to the father and not want him to be hurt; as one victim said: "I didn't want to have him arrested. I just wanted him to leave me alone." Or she may not want to wound her mother by telling her. Child-care workers say that most young victims remain silent until they can stand things no longer or become pregnant.

The silence often continues once the mother learns what

is happening. Perhaps she can't believe what she hears—can't imagine that her husband could be guilty of such an outrage. Or she may keep silent out of fear that the husband will run off. Or that he'll be arrested. Or that the family will be broken up. If the word spreads to other relatives, their feelings will likely be much the same—either disbelief or fear that the family will be broken up and publicly humiliated.

Many families deeply fear the harm that can be done to the victim if a report is made. Just as in other sexual abuses, there can be police questions that embarrass, frighten, or humiliate the child. There can be an arrest. There can be a separation from the family, with the child being placed in a foster home. And there can be a trial.

The trouble that started all this was bad enough in itself and may take the child years to forget. But the resulting investigation can make the forgetting twice as hard.

TOWARD A SOLUTION

Because so little has been known about incest, the work of helping the victims and the families caught up in it has been slow in starting.

But the work is now under way. As we have discussed, police departments across the country have put together special units that can handle any sexual abuse cases with sympathy and tact. Likewise, hospitals and public agencies are now instructing their staffs in how to treat incest and other sexual abuse problems with greater skill.

Taking shape also are programs that can be of help. They are as yet few in number. One of the finest is the Child Sexual Abuse Treatment Program (CSATP) that was mentioned at the start of the chapter.

In working with the incest victim, CSATP uses therapy and counseling. Both are meant to help the child ease and overcome all the anger, revulsion, and shame that he or she may feel. They're also meant to help ease the pain if there has been an arrest and the family is being broken up.

Work with the parents is based on the "new approach" for treating all types of abusers. Through therapy and counseling, the parent or guardian is helped to face up to what he or she has done, to take responsibility for the act, and to rebuild his or her life. Both mother and father are helped to look at and solve the problems that caused the incest.

In addition to all this work, CSATP helps the family through the investigation of the incest and then the ordeal of a trial, should one be held.

The combined therapy and counseling usually lasts from six months to a year. At the finish, the family members may join Daughters United and Parents United. These are self-help organizations that enable the victim and the parents to continue the job of rebuilding their lives and avoiding future trouble.

CSATP has proved a great success. Today, rather than sending some fathers to prison, the local courts refer them to the program for help. When it completed its fifth year of work some time ago, CSATP reported that more than four hundred families had gone through its therapy and counseling. Out of all those families, there were only two reports of new sexual abuse.

As the public learns more and more of the incest problem, it is hoped that programs similar to CSATP will take shape in communities all across the country. Then perhaps incest will no longer be a silent and dreaded crime. Perhaps it will then be known as an illness that—terrible though it is— can be successfully treated.

10
CHILD PORNOGRAPHY

In 1977, Dr. Judianne Densen-Gerber received a shock. It came when she opened a brown paper package that had just arrived in the mail. A psychiatrist and lawyer, Dr. Densen-Gerber is the founder of Odyssey Institute, an organization dedicated to helping socially disadvantaged people.

Inside the package was a magazine called *Moppets*. It was filled with photographs of boys and girls between the ages of three and eight. The doctor's eyebrows went up. The youngsters were all in the nude. Some were performing sex acts with each other. Some were with adults. There was an unsigned note attached. It asked, "Are you aware of this?"

Dr. Densen-Gerber shook her head. Her Odyssey Institute had helped many adult drug abusers. And it had helped all sorts of children in trouble. But, no, she was not aware of *this*. Not aware that children were being used as models for pornographic materials. She decided to make herself aware —immediately.

Her office is in New York City. She went to the Times

Square area, long a center for the purchase of adult pornography. She later wrote that, in the bookstores there, she bought such magazines as *Lollitots, Nudist Moppets, Naughty Horny Imps,* and *Lust for Children.* All were crammed with photos of children involved in sex acts. The youngsters ranged in age from three to the early teens.

She also found thirty-five short motion pictures featuring children in sexual acts. Sixteen of them were about incest. One showed a "father" and his four-year-old "daughter" engaged in sex.

The doctor later carried her search to other cities. She found the same kind of filth in the "porno shops" of Philadelphia, Washington, D.C., Detroit, Chicago, New Orleans, San Francisco, and Los Angeles. And as far away as the Australian cities of Sydney, Canberra, and Melbourne.

All that she saw infuriated her. The public had to learn of this outrage. And so the doctor held a press conference right in the Times Square area. Then she went to Washington, D.C., for another press conference.

A shock wave rolled across the country when Dr. Denson-Gerber's findings were reported in the newspapers and on television. We Americans knew that child abuse was a growing menace. Now, appalled, we learned that something new had been added to the problem—an industry that cold-bloodedly exploited children and made a fortune doing it.

In the next months, we learned even more.

BIG BUSINESS

To begin, we found that child pornography—or "kiddieporn" as it was called—is nothing new. It's been around for centuries, first in paintings and drawings, and then in photographs. But it had never been especially popular in this country. Far more popular among people who liked such things was adult pornography.

Further, most of the kiddieporn that we did have was

not produced here in the United States. It was smuggled in from foreign countries.

But suddenly, in the 1970s, everything began to change. Sales in child pornography boomed. Books, films, and magazines flooded the country. They could be bought at porno shops or from mail-order houses. Soon, more than 260 magazines like *Moppets* and *Lollitots* were on the market. The kiddieporn business mushroomed into a big industry.

It was an industry of enormous profits. Short movies that had been made in a motel room or a garage were being sold—or rented again and again—for prices ranging from twenty-five dollars to several hundred dollars. Magazines that had been produced for pennies each were bringing extravagant prices. Some sold for as much as ten dollars apiece. It was said that the industry was taking in about a half-billion dollars a year.

It was an industry with three big centers—New York City, Chicago, and Los Angeles. The films and magazines were either produced there or received from other towns across the country or from overseas. The three centers then distributed the material throughout the United States and abroad.

And it was an industry that was using American children—both boys and girls. To this day, no one knows how many youngsters were—and are—involved. But it is agreed that the number is up in the thousands.

THE CHILDREN

Who are these children? We've learned that a great many are runaways who find themselves broke, lonely, and hungry in some strange city. Loitering on a street corner or in a bus station, they're easy targets for the pornographer in search of models. Often, they'll agree to pose for five or ten dollars. Some have gone to work for a meal or a room for the night.

One twelve-year-old said that she took a few dollars but would have posed for nothing because the man who approached her had been the first person in weeks to treat her in a friendly fashion.

Some of the runaways are tricked into posing. One eleven-year-old boy met a man who, seeming to feel sorry for him, took him home and said that he could stay there for a while. The next day, the boy accompanied his new "friend" to what the man said would be a children's party. Once there, the boy was forced to take part in sex acts with the other "guests" while a camera clicked steadily in a corner of the room.

It's been estimated that, at most times, there are about a million runaways in the United States. They constitute a great "labor pool" for the pornographer. So great is it that pornographers always have "scouts" working big-city bus stations, railroad depots, and airports. They search out and then recruit any likely looking youngsters arriving in town.

The situation with the runaways is bad enough. But there's something else that strikes most people as being even worse. Some children are sold into the kiddieporn business by their parents or guardians.

For instance, an Illinois man was sent to jail in 1976 for hiring his three foster sons out to a photographer. He allowed them to be photographed while performing various sex acts. He was paid $150 for each boy. A Colorado couple received $3,000 for the use of their son.

Three prostitute mothers were arrested in Los Angeles recently. They had rented out their children for kiddieporn pictures. The victims were a three-year-old girl, a five-year-old girl, and a ten-year-old boy. In Los Angeles and several other cities, drug addicts have been arrested for the same thing. Their price: enough for a fix.

Some parents have even gone into the kiddieporn business themselves. Police report that, in a number of families where there is incest, the parents will have themselves photographed with their children. They'll then sell the pictures to other parents or to porno magazines.

Some people who are charged with the care of children have also gone into the business. Tennessee was shocked recently when a minister who ran a farm for neglected boys was taken into custody. Police arrested him for having the boys engage in homosexual acts while he photographed them. He then sent the pictures to customers in various parts of the country.

The whole business of child pornography has sickened every thoughtful American. The acts are vicious and the damage done to the children great. The victims suffer all the fright and humiliation of every other abused child. Further, psychiatrists believe that they soon lose their self-esteem and come to see themselves not as worthwhile human beings but as merchandise meant to be used and sold.

These feelings can follow them through the years, perhaps making it impossible for them ever to live happy and normal lives. There is also the great possiblity that, raised in sexual cruelty, they themselves will become sexually abusive parents. A terrible tradition will have been started.

The whole business, too, has been a puzzle to thoughtful Americans. Why, they've asked, has the kiddieporn industry grown so quickly? Why are there so many ready customers for it? Why do some parents send their children into it?

An entire book could be written in trying to answer these questions. The best we can do in just one chapter is come up with several general answers.

THE CUSTOMERS

So far as the customers are concerned, let's simply say that every society has always had its share of sick people who take pleasure and excitement in evil. In this instance, it's the evil of looking at a child being used as a sexual toy.

There was a time when kiddieporn appealed to just a few lost souls—men who were usually described as "weirdos" or "dirty old men." But a new and different type of customer has joined them.

The New York City police, in a recent study of kiddieporn, had undercover officers run a porno bookshop in the Times Square area for several months. They found that a large percentage of the customers were well-dressed businessmen. Most wore suits and ties and carried attaché cases. They were obviously family men from middle-class and upper-class neighborhoods.

Why these new customers? Some experts blame the pressures and problems of our times. As was mentioned in chapter 2, these pressures and problems have caused many parents to strike out at their children. They seem to have caused others to seek escape—escape into sexual fantasies involving children.

One problem has been singled out for special blame. Sex has become a sensational thing. It's sensationalized in everything from magazines to television. All of this has caused a growing number of people to become jaded. What excited them last month or last year no longer excites them. They keep looking for stranger and stranger thrills. The pornographers—cold-blooded businessmen who have been working for centuries—have found a new thrill for them in children.

ATTACKING THE PROBLEM

As soon as the mushrooming problem of kiddieporn came to light, an angry public called for action.

Some of the first moves against the problem were made by the state governments. Years ago, just a handful of states carried laws that had anything to do with child pornography. But—with Arizona, Minnesota, and Tennessee taking the lead—more than twenty states soon passed laws that made it a felony to use children for pornographic purposes. As this book is being written, at least eleven more states are considering similar laws.

There was also action at the federal level. By mid-1977, just a few short months after Dr. Densen-Gerber's press conferences, no fewer than twenty Senators and one hundred members of the House of Representatives were calling for measures against kiddieporn. One proposal wanted to outlaw the photographing of children under sixteen years in sexual acts. The penalty would be imprisonment up to twenty years and fines up to $50,000.

The Congress and the various state legislatures found themselves up against a constitutional debate as they began considering kiddieporn laws. There was the question of whether any of the laws would violate the First Amendment of the Constitution, which guarantees freedom of speech and of the press.

The feeling was that the laws could move against the people who recruited the children and the people who produced the pornography. But what was produced—the material itself—was constitutionally protected, no matter how onerous it might be. Likewise, it was felt that laws against the distributors and sellers of kiddieporn would be in violation of the First Amendment.

Though they hated the very idea of kiddieporn, many people and organizations—among them the American Civil Liberties Union—felt that the laws must not be allowed to trample on the First Amendment. Were they to do so, they might well open the door to future moves against serious works of literature, art, and the theater that deal with sexual themes—or with any other theme that some segment of the public decided that it didn't like. Serious works had to be protected against censorship at all costs.

Even now, there is debate over whether some of the

new state laws are constitutional. The same applies to some of the laws now being considered by other states for future passage.

Throughout 1977, a number of kiddieporn bills were presented in Congress. Out of them came a new law. It was enacted in early 1978 and is titled the Protection of Children Against Sexual Abuse Act. It is a measure that deals only with pornographic material that is carried, shipped, or mailed between the states or sent to foreign countries. This keeps it from interfering with the individual state laws.

The law says, first, that no person—photographer, parent, guardian, or anyone else—may hire, use, or permit a minor to engage in any sexual act for material that will then travel between the states or be sent overseas.

Likewise, no one may mail, carry, or ship between the states—or send overseas—any material that shows a minor engaged in sexual conduct. Nor may anyone receive such material.

The act calls for violations to be punished by a prison sentence and/or a fine. A first violation brings a $10,000 fine and/or a sentence of up to ten years. Further violations result in a $15,000 fine and/or a sentence of up to twenty years.

The act also outlaws the transporting of girls under eighteen across state lines for pornographic purposes, among them prostitution. Violations are punishable by a $10,000 fine and/or prison terms up to ten years.

WHERE DO WE STAND NOW?

The new laws and the public's outrage have hurt the kiddieporn industry. There have been police crackdowns and citizen demonstrations that have forced some of the porno shops to close or get rid of the child material. But too many of the closings have been temporary. Too much of the material has returned to the display shelves. Though hurt, the industry continues to thrive.

The people who are leading the fight to crush the market say that the new laws are helpful but not strong enough. They want to see kiddieporn laws in all states.

Dr. Densen-Gerber is urging that the states require that all media in which children appear be licensed; that the children be prohibited from performing sexual acts for them; and that any material in violation be taken over immediately by the authorities and destroyed.

She also wants to see all child abuse and neglect laws broadened to include sexual exploitation. And she wants to see all obscenity laws carry greater penalties for offensive material involving children under sixteen.

She urges people to write their state and federal legislators, asking that they press for these measures. And she continues to urge everyone to work toward building a sense of unity and closeness in the home. It's the unity and closeness that add up to love. It's found in those countless American families where the children are cherished and not mistreated.

In the long run, it's the best way not only to solve the child pornography problem, but to end child abuse in all its forms.

A SELECTED
READING LIST

If you're interested in studying more about the child-abuse problem, you'll find the following books and magazine articles to be of particular help:

BOOKS

DeCouray, Peter and DeCouray, Judith, *A Silent Tragedy: Child Abuse in the Community*. Port Washington, N.Y.: Alfred Publishing Co., 1973.

Fontana, Vincent J. *Somewhere a Child Is Crying*. New York: Macmillan, 1973.

Ginott, Haim G. *Between Parent and Child*. New York: Macmillan, 1965.

Helfer, Ray, and Kempe, C. Henry. *The Battered Child*. Chicago: University of Chicago Press, 1968.

James, Howard. *Children in Trouble: A National Scandal*. New York: David McKay Co., 1969.

Wilkerson, David. *Parents on Trial.* New York: Pyramid Publications, 1970.

Young, Leontine. *Wednesday's Children.* New York: Mc-Graw-Hill, 1964.

MAGAZINE ARTICLES

Anderson, George. "Child Abuse," *America,* May 28, 1977.

Bridge, Peter. "What Parents Should Know About 'Kiddie Porn.'" *Parent's Magazine,* January 1978.

Densen-Gerber, Judianne. "What Pornographers Are Doing to Children: A Shocking Report." *Redbook,* August 1977.

Dudar, Helen. "America Discovers Child Pornography." *Ms,* August 1977.

Kaul, Mohan L. "Physical Child Abuse and Its Prevention." *Intellect,* February 1977.

Newsweek. "The Battered Child." October 10, 1977.

Remsburg, Charles, and Remsburg, Bonnie. "An American Scandal: Why Some Parents Abuse Their Teens." *Seventeen,* May 1977.

Schultz, Dodi. "The Terror of Child Molestation." *Parent's Magazine,* February 1977.

Time. "Child's Garden of Perversity." April 4, 1977.

U.S. News & World Report, "Authorities Face Up to the Child-Abuse Problem." May 3, 1976.

————. "Child Pornography: Outrage Starts to Stir Some Action." June 13, 1977.

Weber, Ellen. "Incest: Sexual Abuse Begins at Home." *Ms,* April 1977.

INDEX